CALVARY'S CROSS

A Symposium on the Atonement

"Having made Peace through the Blood of His Cross."—Col. 1:20

❧

Fredonia Books
Amsterdam. The Netherlands

Calvary's Cross

by
Moody, Talmage, Spurgeon, et al

ISBN: 1-58963-330-X

Copyright © 2001 by Fredonia Books

Reprinted from the 1900 edition

Fredonia Books
Amsterdam, The Netherlands
http://www.fredoniabooks.com

JESUS ON THE CROSS.

CONTENTS

CONTENTS

"THE MAN THAT DIED FOR ME"

By MRS. J. K. BARNEY

Many years ago I wanted to go as a foreign missionary, but my way seemed hedged about. After a few years I went to live on the Pacific coast. Life was rough in the mining country where I lived, and this was my chance for missionary work.

I heard of a man over the hills who was dying of consumption. "He is so vile," they said, "no one can stand it to stay with him; so the boys place food by him and leave him for twenty-four hours. They'll find him dead sometime, and the quicker the better. Never had a soul, I guess."

The pity of it haunted me as I went about my work, and I tried for three days to get some one to go and see him and find out if he was in need of better care. As I turned from the last man, vexed with his indifference, the thought came to me:

"Why don't you go yourself? Here's missionary work, if you want it."

I'll not tell how I weighed the probable usefulness of my going, or how I shrank from one so vile as he. It wasn't the kind of work I wanted.

At last one day I went over the hills to the little mud cabin. It was just one room. The door stood open, and up in one corner on some straw and colored blankets I found the dying man. Sin had left awful marks on his

7

face, and if I had not heard that he could not move, I should have fled.

As my shadow fell over the floor he looked up and greeted me with a dreadful oath.

"Don't speak so, my friend," I said.

"I ain't your friend," he said. "I never had any friends, and I don't want any now."

I reached out, at arm's length, the fruit I had brought him, and stepping back to the doorway I asked him, hoping to find a tender place in his heart, if he remembered his mother, but he cursed her. I asked him if he ever had a wife, and he cursed her. I spoke of God, and he cursed Him. I tried to speak of Jesus and His death for us, but he stopped me with his oaths, and said:

"That's all a lie. Nobody ever died for others."

I went away discouraged. I said to myself:

"I knew it was no use."

But the next day I went again, and every day for two weeks, but he did not show the gratitude of a dog. At the end of that time I said:

"I'm not going any more."

That night, when I was putting my little boys to bed, I did not pray for the miner, as I had been accustomed to do. My little Charlie noticed it and said:

"Mamma, you did not pray for the bad man."

"No," I answered with a sigh.

"Have you given him up, mamma?"

"Yes, I guess so."

"Has God given him up, mamma?"

That night I could not sleep "The man dying, and so vile, with no one to care!"

I got up and went away by myself to pray, but as my

knees touched the floor I was overpowered by the sense
of how defective had been my prayers. I had had no
faith, and I had not really cared, beyond a half-hearted
sentiment. Oh, the shame, the sham, of my missionary
zeal! I fell on my face literally, as I cried:

"Oh, Christ, give me a little glimpse of the worth of
a human soul."

I stayed on my knees until Calvary became a reality
to me. I cannot describe those hours. They came and
went unheeded, but I learned that night what I had
never known before, what it is to travail for a human
soul. I saw my Lord that night as I had never seen
Him before.

The next morning brought a lesson in Christian work
I had never learned before. I had waited on other days
until the afternoon, when, my work being all over, I
could change my dress, put on my gloves, and take a
walk while the shadows were on the hillsides. That
day, the moment my little boys went off to school I
left my work, and hurried over the hills, not to see "that
vile wretch," but to win a soul. There was a human
soul in the balance, and I wanted to get there quickly.
As I passed on, a neighbor come out of her house and
said:

"I'll go over the hills with you, I guess."

I did not want her, but it was another lesson for me.
God could plan better than I could. She had her little
girl with her. As we reached the cabin she said:

"I'll wait out here; and you'll hurry, won't you?"

I do not know what I expected, but the man greeted
me with an awful oath. It did not hurt me as it did
before, for I was behind Christ, and I stayed there. I
could bear what struck Him first.

While I was changing the basin of water and towel for him, things which I had done every day, and which he had used but never thanked me for, the clear laugh of the little girl rang out upon the air like a bird's note.

"What's that?" said the man eagerly.

"It's a little girl outside who is waiting for me."

"Would you mind letting her in?" he said, in a different tone from any I had heard before.

Stepping to the door I beckoned to her, and then taking her by the hand, said:

"Come in and see the sick man, Mamie."

She shrank back as she saw his face and said:

"I'se 'fraid."

But I assured her with, "Poor sick man! he can't get up, and he wants to see you."

She looked like an angel, with her face framed in golden curls, her eyes tender and pitiful, and in her hand the flowers she had picked from the purple sage brush. Bending towards him she said:

"I sorry for 'ou, sick man. Will 'ou have a posy?"

He laid his great bony hand beyond the flowers on the plump hand of the child, and tears came to his eyes, as he said:

"I had a little girl once, and she died. Her name was Mamie. She cared for me. Nobody else did. Guess I'd been different if she'd lived. I've hated everybody since she died."

I knew at once I had the key to the man's heart, and the thought came quickly, born of that midnight prayer service:

"When I spoke of your mother and your wife you cursed them, and I know now that they were not good women or you could not have done it."

"Good women! Oh, you don't know about that kind of women. You can't think what they was."

"Well, if your little girl had lived and grown up with them, wouldn't she have been just like them? You would not have liked to have her live for that, would you?"

He evidently had not thought of this, and his great eyes looked off for a full minute. As they came back to mine he cried:

"Oh, no! no! I'd killed her first. I'm glad she died."

Reaching out and taking the poor hand I said:

"The dear Lord didn't want her to be like them. He loved her better than you did. So He took her away where she could be cared for by the angels. He is keeping her for you. To-day she is waiting for you. Don't you want to see her again?"

"Oh, I'd be willing to be burned alive a thousand times over if I could just see my little gal once more, my little Mamie."

Oh, what a blessed story I had to tell that hour, and I had been so close to Calvary that night that I could tell it in earnest!

The poor face grew ashy pale as I talked, and the man threw up his arms as though his agony was mastering him. Two or three times he gasped as though losing breath. Then clutching me he said:

"What is that, woman, you said t'other day about talkin' to somebody out 'o sight?"

"It's praying. I tell God what I want."

"Pray now! pray quick! Tell Him I want my little gal again. Tell Him anything you want to."

I took the hands of the child and placed them on the trembling hand of the man. Then dropping on my

knees, with the child in front of me, I bade her pray
for the man who had lost his little Mamie and wanted
to see her again. As nearly as I remember, this was
Mamie's prayer:

"Dear Jesus, this man is sick. He has lost his 'ittle
girl, and he feels bad about it. I'se so sorry for him,
and he's sorry too. Won't you help him, and show him
where to find his 'ittle girl? Do, please. Amen."

Heaven seemed to open before us. There stood One
with the prints of the nails in His hands and the
wounds in His side.

Mamie slipped away soon, but the man kept saying:
"Tell Him more about it, tell Him everything—but
oh! you don't know."

Then he poured out such a torrent of confession that
I could not have borne it but for the One that was
close to us that hour, reaching out after that lost soul.

It was the third day when the poor, tired soul turned
from everything to Him, the Mighty to save, "The
Man that died for me."

He lived on for four weeks, as if God would show
how real was the change. I had been telling him one
day about a meeting, and he said:

"I'd like to go to meetin' once. I never went to one
of them things."

So we planned a meeting, and the boys came from
the mills and the mines, and filled the room.

"Now, boys," said he, "get down on your knees
while she tells about that Man that died for me."

I had been brought up to believe that a woman
shouldn't speak in meeting, but I found myself talking,
and I tried to tell the simple story of the Cross.

After a while he said, "Oh, boys, you don't half believe it, or you'd cry; you couldn't help it. Boys, raise me up. I'd like to tell it once.''

So they raised him up, and between his short breathing and coughing he told the story, and this, as well as I can recall, is a part of what he said:

''Boys,'' he said, ''you know how the water runs down the sluice-boxes and carries off all the dirt and leaves the gold behind. Well, the blood of that Man she tells about went right over me just like that; it carried off 'bout everything. But it left enough for me to see Mamie, and to see the Man that died for me. Oh, boys, can't you love Him?''

Some days after, I saw that the end was near, and as I left him I said:

''What shall I say to-night, Jack?''

''Just 'Good-night,' '' he said, ''and when we meet again I'll say 'Good-morning' up there.''

The next morning the door was closed, and I found two men sitting silently by a board stretched across two stools. They turned back the sheet, and I looked on the face of the dead, which seemed to have come back nearer to the ''image of God.''

''I wish you could have seen him when he went,'' they said. ''He brightened up 'bout midnight, an' smiling said, 'I'm going, boys. Tell her I am going to see Mamie. Tell her I'm going to see the Man that died for me'; and he was gone.''

THE BLOOD

By D. L. MOODY

PART I.—THE OLD TESTAMENT

"It is the blood that maketh an atonement for the soul."

LEV. xvii. 11.

Every man should be able to give a reason for the hope that is in him; and I do not believe the man lives who can give a reason for his hope beyond the grave, who is a stranger to the blood of Christ. I am often told that I make the plan of salvation too easy, and that it is folly to say that men can be saved by trusting simply to His atoning blood. I do not wish any one to believe what I say, if it is not according to Scripture; and the best way is just to turn up the Bible and see what it says.

The first portion of Scripture I would call your attention to is from the very first book of the Bible. In Genesis iii. 21, you find:

"Unto Adam also and to his wife did the Lord God make coats of skins, and clothed them."

In this verse we get the first glimpse of blood. Certainly God could not have clothed Adam and Eve with the skins of beasts unless He had shed blood. It was a case of the innocent slain for the guilty. It may be that this was a type, away back in Eden, of Christ, the coming One, of the Sacrifice to be slain; and Adam might have said to his wife:

"Well, even though God has driven us out of Eden, He loves us, and this coat is a token of His love."

Some one has said God put a lamp of promise into his hand before He drove him out: "The seed of the woman shall bruise the head of the serpent."

To me it is a very sweet thought that sin was covered before Adam was driven out of Eden—that God dealt in grace with him before He dealt in judgment. Did you ever think what a terrible state of things it would be if man in his lost and ruined state were allowed to live forever? It was from love to Adam that God drove him out of Eden, that he should not live for ever. God put the cherubim there with the flaming sword. But now Christ has come and taken the sword into His own bosom, and opened wide the gates, so that man can come in and eat. Adam might have been in Eden ten thousand years and then be led astray by Satan; but now "our life is hid with Christ in God." Yes, man is safer with the second Adam out of Eden than with the first Adam in Eden.

MAN'S WAY AND GOD'S WAY

Then let us turn to Genesis iv. 4: "And Abel, he also brought of the firstlings of his flock, and of the fat thereof. And the Lord had respect unto Abel and to his offering; but unto Cain and to his offering he had not respect."

Now here were two boys who were born and brought up outside of Eden. They were children of the same parents, and brought up under precisely similar circumstances and under the same influences, and there is no account of any difference between these two boys until they go to offer sacrifice. Abel brings the blood, and is accepted; Cain comes in his own way, and is rejected.

Undoubtedly, when our first parents fell, God marked out the way by which man might come to Him; Abel walked in God's way, but Cain in his own. You may have wondered why Cain's offering was not just as acceptable to Him as Abel's; but one took God's way and the other took his own. Perhaps Cain said he could not bear the sight of blood, and took that which God had *cursed,* and laid it on the altar. Perhaps he said to himself:

"I shall certainly not bring a bleeding lamb. I don't like that doctrine at all. Here is the grain and the beautiful fruit which I have raised by my industry, and I'm sure it looks better than blood."

And there are a great many Cainites in the church to-day. They are trying to get into heaven their own way. They bring their own good deeds to God. They prefer what is agreeable to the eye, as Cain did his beautiful corn and fruit; but they do not like the doctrine of the Blood of the Atonement. From the time Adam left Eden there have been Abelites and Cainites. The Abelites come by way of the blood—the Cainites come in a way of their own. They wish to get rid of the doctrine of the blood. But be assured that any religion which makes light of the blood is of the devil. No matter how eloquent a man is, if he preaches against the blood he is doing the devil's work. Do not listen to him. Do not believe him. If an angel from heaven should preach any other gospel I would not believe it. "Christ died for our sins,"—that is the Gospel that Paul preached, and Peter preached, and that God has always honored in the salvation of men's soul's.

Come down the stream of time 2,000 years, and you find another important event. Genesis viii. 20: "And

Noah builded an altar unto the Lord; and took of every clean beast, and of every clean fowl, and offered burnt offerings on the altar.''

We have now passed out of the first dispensation and have come to the second; and the very first thing Noah does, is to put blood between him and his sins. The second dispensation is founded upon blood. Thus Noah walked by the highway of the blood; for this the animals were taken through the flood; and all God's people have been walking that way since, for it is the blood that atones for sin.

Would you turn to Genesis xxii. 13? ''And Abraham lifted up his eyes and looked, and behold, behind him a ram caught in a thicket by his horns. And Abraham, went and took the ram and offered him up for a burnt offering in the stead of his son.''

God loved Abraham so much that He spared his son, but He so loved the world that He did not spare His own Son, but delivered Him up for us all. Now we are told that Abraham saw Christ's day and was glad. I do not know when he saw it, but I have an idea that it was from this very place that God drew back the curtain of time and showed him Christ as the bearer of sin.

Just look at that scene. There is the altar, built at the command of Jehovah. God had told him to take his son, his only son whom he loved, and bind and slay him. He has bound the boy. Everything is ready, and now he takes the knife to slay his son. He does not know what it means, but *God said it*, and he obeys. I wish we had men like Abraham now-a-days, willing to obey God in the dark, not asking the reason why. I can see him put his arms round his boy as he takes him to his bosom and weeps over him. I can hear him tell-

ing him the secret he had hidden from him so long.
What a scene! What a struggle it must have been!

Now he is ready to plunge the knife into the heart of
his son. But hark! there comes a voice from heaven:
"Abraham, Abraham! spare thy son."

Ah! there was no voice at Calvary, no cry from heaven
then, "Spare thy Son." He gave him up freely for us
all, the Innocent for the guilty, the Just for the unjust.

THE SPRINKLED BLOOD

Turn now to Exodus xii.—one of the most important
chapters in the Old Testament, where God puts the
whole nation of Israel behind blood. At the 13th
verse we read, "And the blood shall be to you for a
token upon the houses where ye are; and when I see the
blood I will pass over you, and the plague shall not be
upon you to destroy you."

God did not say, "When I see your good deeds—how
you have prayed, and wept, and groaned, I will pass
over you," but *"when I see the blood."* It was not
their good resolutions, their tears, their prayers, their
works, their faith, that saved those men in Egypt; it was
the blood. What were they to do to be saved? They
were to put the blood on the door-posts and lintel.

They were not to put it on the threshold. God would
not have them trample upon the blood. But that is
what the world is doing to-day.

Men say it is not the death of Christ; it is His life.
But God did not say, "Take a white, spotless lamb, and
put it there at the front of the door, and when I see the
lamb I will pass over you. Had an Israelite done that,
the angel of death would have passed by the lamb, would
have entered that house, would have laid his cold hand

on the eldest born. A live lamb could not have kept death out that night; he would have fallen a victim like the Egyptian.

Very likely, when some of the lords and dukes and great men rode through Goshen, and saw the Israelites sprinkling their dwellings, they said they never saw such foolishness. Very likely they thought they were just spoiling their houses. Every house had blood upon it. No Egyptian could understand it. But on that memorable night when Death entered every house from the palace of the king to the hovel of the poor, when the wail of sorrow went up from that stricken land, it was the blood that kept him from the homes of Goshen. Yes, it is the blood that must cover our sins.

I beg of you, do not let the world move you on this point. Let it go on mocking, and laughing, and making light of the precious blood of the Son of God. It is our only refuge, our only hope. We cannot cover sin by any good deeds of our own.

It is a very common saying, "If I were only as good as that man who has preached the Gospel for fifty years, or that mother in Israel who has visited the sick and been so kind to the poor, I would feel safe for heaven."

But I want to say that if you are sheltered behind the blood of the Son of God, you are as safe as any saint that ever walked this earth. It is not a long life of good deeds that is going to save us. It is not our Christian usefulness that will ever commend us to God. Certainly we must work for Christ; certainly it will be better for you in the future if you do. But that is not salvation. Certainly you must follow Christ; certainly you must imitate His pure and holy life. I would go further, and say it is an *absolute necessity* you should do so; but the life of Christ may be preached forever, and if His death be left out, it will never save a soul. People say you must work, work, work, in order to get salvation. Ten thousand times no! You get it as a gift; "Whosoever will, *let him take.*" You can work as much as you like after you have taken it. "Work out your own salvation." Yes, but that was spoken to Christians, people who had it. So we must first take the gift and then we can work it out. We take salvation as a gift and then begin to work because we cannot help it. All work done before that must go for nothing. When the angel of death swept through the land that night, the good and the bad were destroyed together. Into every house where the blood was not sprinkled, the destroying angel came; but wherever the blood was on door-post or lintel, whether they had worked much, or whether they had worked none, God passed them over.

The little child in the humblest tent was just as safe as Moses or Aaron, as Joshua or Caleb, as safe as any in the land. God did not say, "When I see your gilded palace, or your beautiful home; when I see your goodness, your life of service, or your faith," but, "When I see the blood, *it* shall be a token. Not for their own sakes, but for Christ's, did He pass them by that night. Some one has said that the little fly in Noah's ark was just as safe as the great elephant. It was that ark that saved them both. So Christ saves the weak disciple just as well as the strong one.

When you go to a railway station you find all classes of people wishing to travel. They have their tickets and take their places in the cars. When the conductor comes to ask for the tickets, he does not look to see what or who you are. You may be rich or poor, learned or unlearned, this or that; he looks for the *tickets,* and if you have your ticket you pass. The ticket is the *token.* So if you are sheltered behind the blood of Christ, you may be very ignorant or poor in this world, but you are as safe as the wisest or wealthiest.

A great many people are wondering why they are so weak; why they fall so often when temptation comes, why so little spiritual power is given them. I think you will find a lesson in that same chapter, in the 11th verse:

"Thus shall ye eat it; with your loins girded, your shoes on your feet, and your staff in your hand; and ye shall eat it in haste: it is the Lord's Passover."

They were not only to kill the lamb and take the blood and sprinkle it on the door-posts, but they were to *eat* of it. That is the way to get spiritual strength. The reason why we are such sickly Christians, is because we do not feed on the Lamb. We have a wilderness journey before us as the children of Israel had, and if we do not feed upon Christ we must starve by the way. We have not only to look to the blood for safety, but we must feed on Christ for strength. How much the soul needs to be fed! The Lord has given Him up for us; He calls Himself the Bread of Life. Feeding upon Christ is feeding on His Word. There is no book that will feed the soul but the Bible. If I feed on the Word of God, I get spiritual strength and power. Some people think if they get one glimpse at Christ it is enough. We must live by faith as well as be saved by faith. The just shall live by faith.

In verse 2 we read, "This month shall be unto you the beginning of months. It shall be the first month of

the year to you.'' For 400 years they had been serving
the king of the Egyptians, but God would not let them
count those years. They must make a fresh start, as it
were. So all the years that we spend in the service of
the devil go for naught. Life never really begins until
we have been sprinkled with the blood of Christ.
Everything dates from the blood, and even the Jew has
to own that the death upon the cross was the beginning
of days.

Turn now to Exodus xxix. 16: "And thou shalt slay
the ram, and thou shalt take his blood and sprinkle it
round about upon the altar.''

I used to read these words of the Old Testament, wondering what they meant. They were to take the blood
and sprinkle it "round about upon the altar.'' Now I
think I understand it. It teaches that there is no way
of approaching God without coming by the blood. It
has been so in all ages. Even Aaron, the high priest,
had to take blood and sprinkle it round about upon the
altar, before he could have an interview with God—
teaching us the great lesson that approach to God never
has been, never will be, never can be, except through
the blood of the Lamb.

We have the same thing brought before us again in
the 10th verse of the 30th chapter: "And Aaron shall
make an atonement upon the horns of the altar, once
in a year, with the blood of the sin offering of atone-
ments; once in the year shall he make atonement upon
it throughout your generations: it is most holy unto
the Lord.''

Atonement means at-one-ment; the blood of Christ
makes the sinner and God at one. Before Adam fell,
God had bound him to the throne with a golden chain,

which was broken by the fall, but Christ came down and linked man back to God again. *At-one-ment*—that is what the blood of Christ does; it makes atonement. We talk about sins being forgiven; they are forgiven, but no sin ever committed in this world was forgiven without being punished. They were punished in Christ; He made expiation—"Who His own self bare our sins in His own body on the tree." Think what it cost Christ to make expiation. Think what it cost God when He had to give up His only begotten Son, to give Him up to die!

Turn for a moment to Leviticus viii. 23: "And he slew it, and Moses took of the blood of it and put it upon the tip of Aaron's right ear, and upon the thumb of his right hand, and upon the great toe of his right foot."

That is another verse I used to stumble over. What did it mean, blood on the ear, blood on the hand, blood on the foot? I think I understand it now.

Blood on the ear—without it man cannot hear the voice of God. No uncircumcised ear can hear His voice. Men heard the voice of God and said it thundered; they did not know the difference. But when the blood is applied, men know the voice of God—we know that it is the voice of our loving Father in heaven.

Blood on the hand—that a man may work for God. Those men that think they are working for God, and yet ignore the blood, are deceiving their own souls. One day they will wake up to find that their labor is in vain. Salvation is *"to him that worketh not* but believeth." No man can work his way into the kingdom of God. They said to Christ, "What shall we do that we may work the works of God?" Perhaps these men had got their pockets full of money, and were ready and willing to build churches. "This is the work of God," said Christ, "that ye believe on Him whom He hath sent." No man or woman can do anything to please God until they have believed on His Son.

Blood upon the foot—to walk with God. God never walked with the Israelites until the blood was sprinkled in Goshen. Then nothing could stand before them. When they came to the Red Sea, it fled at their approach. In the wilderness He opened His hand and gave them manna to eat. When they came to Jordan they walked dry-shod through the bed of the river, because the Almighty God was walking beside them. Yes, it was a blood-bought people that God brought into Canaan, the promised land. And God will walk with every blood-washed sinner, and no man shall stand before Him.

WHY GOD DEMANDS BLOOD

I can imagine some of you saying, "I do not understand yet why God demands blood." A person said to me, "I hate your God, your God demands blood. I don't believe in such a God. My God is merciful to all; I do not know your God."

But if you will turn to Leviticus xvii. 11, you will find why God demands blood. "For the life of the flesh is in the blood; and I have given it to you upon the altar to make an atonement for your souls; for it is the blood that maketh an atonement for the soul."

Suppose the governor of your state did not like any man to be deprived of his liberty, and threw all the prisons open, and was so merciful that he could not bear any one to suffer for guilt, how long would he hold the office? How long would he be governor? Not twenty-

four hours. Those very men who cry out about God
being merciful would say, "We don't want such a governor. Well, God is merciful, but he is not going to
taken an unpardoned sinner into heaven.

God demands blood because He said to Adam, "In
the day that thou eatest thereof thou shalt surely die."
But Satan said to Adam and Eve that it was a lie, and
thus there was a controversy between God and Satan,
and, my friends, that controversy has been going on ever
since, and it isn't settled yet. I can go out on the
streets to-day and find men living in sin and abomina-
tion, and if I tell them, "The wages of sin is death,"
they reply, "It's not so; it's a lie."

Sin came into the world and brought death in. God's
word must be kept. How could God do this and spare
the sinner? How could God be just, and justify the
ungodly? Man has sinned and man must die. But
what if some one should die instead of him? His own
life has been forfeited—the wages of sin is *death*—but
what if some one should *buy it back* for him, should *redeem* him? What if one should come forward and lay
down his own life a ransom for many—one who had no
sins of his own to condemn him to death? Glory to
God in the highest! "God so loved the world, that He
gave His only begotten Son, that whosoever believeth in
Him should not perish, but have everlasting life."
Glory to God in the highest! He sent His Son, born of
a woman, to take our nature and die in our stead, tast-
ing death for every man. Glory to God in the highest!
"The blood of Jesus Christ His Son cleanseth us from
all sin." If you read your Bible carefully, you will see
the scarlet thread running right through every page.
The blood commences to flow in Genesis, and runs on to

Revelation. That is what God's Book is written for. Take out the scarlet thread, and it would not be worth carrying home.

Three times in this chapter it is repeated, that the life of the flesh is in the blood. Take the blood out of my body, and my life goes out. When God demands blood, in other words He demands life. It has been forfeited. We have sinned, and come short of the glory of God. I must die for my sins, or find some substitute to die in my stead. I cannot get this man or that man to die for me, because they have sinned themselves, and would have to die for their own sins. But Christ was without sin, and therefore He could be my substitute. Here comes in the glorious doctrine of substitution. Christ died for our sins, for mine; and because He died for me, I love Him. Because He died for me I will serve Him, I will work for Him, I will give Him my very life. He robbed death of its sting, and the grave of its victory. Oh! is it not the least we can do to give our poor lives to Him?

When I was in London some years ago, a body of ministers assembled, and they said to me:

"Mr. Moody, we wish you would write out your creed for us."

"It's already in print," I said.

"Where?"

"In the 53d chapter of Isaiah," I replied. "It was written two thousand years ago, but it is as true to-day as when it was written."

My friends, I have not been able to improve on it, I accept it and believe it just as it is. "He was wounded for our transgressions, He was bruised for our iniquities: the chastisement of our peace was upon

Him; and with His stripes we are healed. All we like sheep have gone astray; we have turned every one to his own way; and the Lord HATH laid on Him the iniquity of us all.'' The Bible is all one book. You find the prophets believe this story of the blood. Go into the prophecy of Daniel and what do you find? "He shall be cut off, not for His sins, but for the sins of His people.'' Here you have the mighty doctrine of substitution again.

When the California gold fever broke out, a man went there, leaving his wife in New England with his boy. As soon as he was successful he was to send for them. It was a long time before he succeeded, but at last he got money enough to send for them. The wife's heart leaped for joy. She took her boy to New York, got on board a Pacific steamer, and sailed away to San Francisco. They had not been long at sea before the cry of "Fire!" "Fire!" rang through the ship, and rapidly it gained on them. There was a powder magazine on board, and the captain knew the moment the fire reached the powder, every man, woman and child must perish. They got out the life-boats, but they were too small! In a minute they were overcrowded. The last one was just pushing away, when the mother pled with them to take her and her boy.

"No," they said, "we have got as many as we can hold."

She entreated them so earnestly, that at last they said they would take one more. Do you think she leaped into that boat and left her boy to die? No! She seized her boy, gave him one last hug, kissed him, and dropped him over into the boat.

"My boy," she said, "if you live to see your father, tell him that I died in your place."

That is a faint type of what Christ has done for us. He laid down His life for us, He died that we might live. Now will you not love Him? What would you say of that young man if he should speak contemptuously of such a mother? She went down to a watery grave to save her son. Well, shall we speak contemptuously of such a Savior. Oh, may God make us loyal to Christ! My friends, you will need Him one day. You will need Him when you come to cross the swellings of Jordan. You will need Him when you stand at the bar of God. May God forbid that when death draws nigh it should find you making light of the precious blood of Christ!

THE BLOOD

PART II.—THE NEW TESTAMENT

"Without shedding of blood is no remission."—Heb. ix. 22.

I remember when Mr. Sankey and myself came back to this country in '75, I got a letter from a lady stating that she had read about our work in Europe and was greatly encouraged, and thought we were going to be used in this country, but she had read one of my sermons on the atonement and had given up hope. She said: "Where did Jesus Christ ever teach men they were saved by His death and suffering? Never, never did He teach it." Do you know what I do when I get this kind of a letter? I get my concordance and topical text-book and go right at it, and I begin to preach more on the atonement than ever; and if I get into any town where they don't believe it, I preach it more than ever. The idea that Christ never taught it! If you will read the Gospels carefully, you will find He didn't teach anything else regarding the way of salvation.

Look at the beginning of His ministry, when He went down to be baptized of John in the Jordan. When He made His appearance, what did John say? "Behold the Lamb of God, which taketh away the sin of the world!" Bible students tell us that from the institution of the Passover not less than quarter of a million lambs were slain annually by the Jews for the Passover supper; yet you never find them spoken of as "lambs," always "the lamb." For fifteen hundred years God had been educating the Jews up to that point, and when John burst upon the nation he cried:

"Behold the Lamb of God, which taketh away the sin of the world."

What did Christ teach Nicodemus? "As Moses lifted up the serpent in the wilderness, even so must the Son of Man be lifted up: that whosoever believeth in Him should not perish, but have eternal life. For God so loved the world that He gave His only begotten Son, that whosoever believeth in Him should not perish, but have everlasting life." He never spoke, I believe, of His death but once when He didn't say He would rise again. A year before He was crucified, He was on His way to Capernaum, and He said to His disciples—you will find it in the 9th chapter of Mark and the 31st verse—"The Son of Man is delivered into the hands of men, and they shall kill Him; and after that He is killed He shall rise the third day. But they understood not that saying, and were afraid to ask Him." That was a year before His death. Then in the 10th chapter of Mark and the 32nd verse it says, "And they were in the way going up to Jerusalem; and Jesus went before them: and they were amazed, and as they followed, they were afraid. And He took again the twelve, and began to tell them what things should happen unto Him, saying, Behold we go up to Jerusalem; and the Son of Man shall be delivered unto the chief priests, and unto the scribes, and they shall condemn Him to death, and shall deliver Him to the Gentiles; and they shall mock Him, and shall scourge Him, and shall spit upon Him, and shall kill Him; and the third day He shall rise again." That doesn't look as if He died as a martyr, as if He didn't come into the world expecting to die for a special purpose. Mark too the account of the transfiguration. That was the most important council ever held on earth. There were present Moses, the great law-giver, and Elijah, the great prophet, and Peter, James and John that became the founders of the new church and the new dispensation, and Jesus, the Son of God, and God the Father. Mark and Matthew leave us in darkness, they don't tell us what they talked about, but Luke does. He says they spoke of "His decease which He should accomplish at Jerusalem." That was the theme that interested heaven, and I believe it is the most important thing to discuss in this world: what Jesus Christ came into this world to do, what He suffered, how He suffered, and what He suffered for.

NOT A MARTYR

Now I want to repudiate the statement that He died as a martyr. People say He laid down certain principles that finally took Him to the cross; that the cross was an accident, He couldn't help it, and He died as a martyr to His principles. Not a word of truth in it! Christ never died as a martyr, and the Bible doesn't say it anywhere. He laid His life down voluntarily. Do you want proof of it? Hear His own words:

"I lay down My life that I might take it again. No man taketh it from Me, but I lay it down of Myself. I have power to lay it down, and I have power to take it again." Jesus Christ could have gone up on the other side of the cross just as well as this side. The law had no claim on Him. If He had broken the law He would have had to die for His own sin, but He was a Lamb without spot or without blemish, and He died as our substitute voluntarily. That is the teaching of Jesus Christ.

When Peter drew his sword and cut off the servant's ear, the Lord rebuked him, and said He could call twelve legions of angels if it was necessary. One angel came and slew 85,000 men; what would 72,000 do? Do you think they had power to arrest the Son of God? Do you think they had power to take Him to Calvary and to His cross? With one wave of His hand He could send them to perdition, the whole of them. All Rome, hell and earth combined couldn't take the life of the Son of God. "I lay down My life, and I take it up again." He voluntarily gave Himself up. He died as your substitute and mine, and that is my hope of heaven. I haven't any other hope; I don't want any other. When people accuse me of preaching an old Gospel, I thank God and take it as a compliment. I do preach an old Gospel. It is 6,000 years old. The Gospel I preach goes back there to Eden.

The 26th of Matthew, 28th verse: "For this is My blood of the new testament, which is shed for many for the remission of sins." Only two of the evangelists record Christ's birth, but all four of them speak of His death and sufferings. Mark says, the 14th chapter and 24th verse: "And He said unto them, This is My blood of the new testament, which is shed for many." Luke xxii. 20: "This cup is the new testament in My blood, which is shed for you."

Then after He had passed through the grave and had risen on the resurrection morn, it says in the 24th of Luke and 26th verse: "Ought not Christ to have suffered these things, and to have entered into His glory? And beginning at Moses and all the prophets, He expounded unto them in all the Scriptures the things concerning Himself." It says in another place He quoted from the Psalms how He was to suffer and how He was to die.

REDEEMED WITH BLOOD

In 1 Peter i. 18, we read: "Forasmuch as ye know that ye were not redeemed with corruptible things, as silver and gold, from your vain conversation, received by tradition from your fathers, but with the precious blood of Christ, as of a lamb without blemish and without spot."

Silver and gold could not redeem our souls. As I have tried to show, life had been forfeited. Death had come into the world by sin, and nothing but blood could atone for the soul. Therefore, says Peter, "You are not redeemed with silver and gold." If gold and silver could have redeemed us, do you not think that God would have created millions of worlds full of gold? It would have been an easy matter for Him. But we are not redeemed by such corruptible things, but by the precious blood of Christ. Redemption means "buying back"; we had sold ourselves for nought, and Christ redeemed us and bought us back.

"How can I be saved?" do you ask. Accept the Redeemer, the Lord Jesus Christ, and rest on His finished work. When Christ on Calvary said "It is finished," it was the shout of a conqueror. He had come to redeem the world, and now He had done it—done it without money! And His cry to the world comes ringing down the ages—"Ho, every one that thirsteth, come ye to the waters; and he that hath no money, come ye, buy and eat; yea, come, buy wine and milk *without money and without price.*"

A few years ago, I was going with a friend to preach one Sunday morning, when a young man drove up in front of us. He had an aged woman with him.

"Who is that young man?" I asked.

"Do you see that beautiful meadow?" said my friend, "and that land there with the house upon it?"

"Yes."

"His father drank that all up," he said. Then he went on to tell all about him. His father was a great drunkard, squandered his property, died, and left his wife in the poor-house. "And that young man," he said, "is one of the finest young men I ever knew. He has toiled hard and earned money, and bought back the land. He has taken his mother out of the poor-house, and now he is taking her to church."

I thought, that is an illustration for me. The first Adam, in Eden, sold us for nought, but the Messiah, the Second Adam, came and bought us back again. The first Adam brought us *to the poor-house,* as it were; the second Adam makes us kings and priests unto God.

That is redemption. We get in Christ all that Adam lost, and more.

Men look on the blood of Christ with scorn and contempt, but the time is coming when the blood of Christ will be worth more than all the kingdoms of the world. Suppose you were going down to death's gates to-night, going down to the brink of the Jordan, without any hope in Christ. Suppose you were a millionaire, what would your millions be worth then? The blood of Christ would be worth more to you than all the silver and gold in the world.

TWO CRIES

The blood has two cries: it cries either for my condemnation (or if you will allow me to use a stronger word, for my damnation), or for my salvation. If I reject the blood of Christ, it cries out for my condemnation; if I accept it, it cries out for pardon and peace. The blood of Abel cried out against his brother Cain. So it was in the days of Christ.

When Pilate had Christ on his hands, he said to the Jews, "What shall I do with Him?" They cried out, "Away with Him! crucify Him!" And when he asked which one he should release, Barabbas or Christ, they cried out, "Barabbas!" Then when he asked again, "What shall I then do with Him?" a universal shout went up from Jerusalem, "Let Him be crucified! Away with Him! We do not want Him." Pilate turned and washed his hands, and said, "I am innocent of this just Man's blood," and they cried, "His blood be on us and on our children. *We* shall take the responsibility of it. *We* endorse the act. Crucify Him, and let His blood be on us and on our children."

Would to God that there might be a cry going up, "Let His blood be on us to save, not to condemn."

PEACE THROUGH THE BLOOD

Turn now to Colossians i. 20: "Having made peace through the blood of His Cross." I can tell you there is no peace in the world. There are many rich men, many great men in the world, who have got no peace. No; I have never seen a man who knew what peace was until he got it at Calvary. "Being justified by faith, we have peace with God through our Lord Jesus Christ" (Rom. v. 1.). Sin covered—that brings peace. There is no peace for the wicked; they are like the troubled sea that cannot rest. Calvary is the place to find peace— peace for the past and grace for the present.

But there is something better still: "And rejoice in hope of the glory of God." Some people think that when they get to Calvary they have got the best; but there is something better in store—glory! I do not know how near it may be to us; it may be that some of us will be ushered very soon into the presence of the King. One gaze at Him will be enough to reward us for all we have had to bear. Yes, there is peace for the past, grace for the present, and glory for the future. These are three things that every child of God ought to have. When the angels came bringing the Gospel, they proclaimed, "Glory to God, peace on earth, and good will towards men." That is what the blood brings—sin covered and taken away, peace for the past, grace for the present, and glory for the future.

Would you now turn to John xix. 34: "But one of the soldiers with a spear pierced His side, and forthwith came there out blood and water."

You know that in Zechariah it was foretold that there should be opened in the house of David a fountain for sin and for uncleanness. Now we have it opened. The Son of God has been pierced by that Roman soldier's spear. It seems to me that that was the crowning act of earth and hell—the crowning act of sin. Look at that Roman soldier as he pushed his spear into the very heart of the God-man. What a hellish deed! But what took place? Blood covered the spear! Oh! thank God, the blood covers sin.

A usurper has got this world now, but Christ will have it soon. The time of our redemption draweth nigh. A little more suffering, and He returns to set up His kingdom and reign upon the earth. He will rend the heavens, and His voice will be heard again. He will descend from heaven with a shout. He will sway His sceptre from the river to the ends of the earth. The thorn and the briar shall be swept away, and the wilderness shall rejoice. Let us rejoice also. We shall see better days. The dreary darkness and sin that sweep along our earth shall be done away with, the dark waves of death and hell shall be beaten back. Oh, let us pray to the Lord to hasten His coming!

Would you now turn to Romans iii. 24: "Being justified freely by His grace, through the redemption that is in Christ Jesus."

What God does He does freely, because He loves to do it. Mark these words, "Through the redemption that is in Christ Jesus." Then in the 5th chapter, 9th verse, we read, "Much more then, being now justified by His blood, we shall be saved from wrath through Him." The sinner is justified with God by His matchless grace through the blood of His Son.

Justified, that means just as if he had never committed sin. What a wonderful thing; not one sin against him! It is as if he owed some one a debt, and when he went to pay it, was told:

"There is nothing against you; it is all settled."

"Why," he would say, "how is that? I got some things from you not long ago, and I want to pay the bill."

"There is nothing against you."

"But I am sure I got something here."

"There is nothing against you in my ledger; some one has come and paid it."

That is substitution. Now I know who paid my spiritual debts. It was the Lord Jesus Christ. God looks at His ledger, and there is nothing against us. Christ was raised up for our justification. It is a good deal better to be justified than pardoned. Suppose I was arrested for stealing $1,000, tried and found guilty; but suppose the judge had mercy on me and pardoned me, I would come out of prison, but it would be with my head down. I had been found guilty, I could never face the world again. But suppose I was accused of stealing and it could not be proven, and when the case came on, it was found I had not done anything of the kind; then I would be *justified*. It would make all the difference in the world. Now God *justifies* us by the blood of His Son. That is what the blood does—sin covered, put out of the way, and nothing against us. Is not that good news?

Revelation i. 5: "Unto Him that loved us and washed us from our sins in His own blood." There are a great many people who wish to be saved, but who think they cannot be saved until they get a little better. If you are going to wait till you get rid of your sins, you will never be saved. You cannot get rid of one sin. Instead of getting better you will get worse. But thanks be to God, He loves us even in our sins, even before He saves us from our sins. "He loved us and washed us from our sins in His own blood." *Loved us* first, then washed us. If we attempt to wash ourselves we will make wretched work of it. The blood will cover it all up if we only trust ourselves to Christ. Who shall lay anything to the charge of God's elect? If He has justified me it is enough.

HYMNS THAT LIVE

Why do we like to sing that old hymn—

> "There is a fountain filled with blood
> Drawn from Immanuel's veins."

Why will it live as long as the church lives on earth? Why do you hear it sung all over Christendom? I remember how it used to thrill my soul even before I was converted. I could not tell why. Thank God, every sin is lost in that fountain. You will find that all these hymns with the scarlet thread in them will live. There is that grand old hymn—

> "Rock of Ages, cleft for me,
> Let me hide myself in Thee;
> Let the water and the blood,
> From Thy riven side that flowed,
> Be of sin the double cure,
> Cleanse me from its guilt and power."

That speaks of the crucified Christ; it will never get worn out. Then there is—

> "Just as I am, without one plea,
> But that Thy blood was shed for me,
> And that Thou bidst me come to Thee
> O Lamb of God. I come."

That is another hymn that will live; you will never tire of it. It will be sung on and on, as long as the church is on earth. I tell you why these are so precious; it is because they tell us about the blood.

Look at Hebrews ix. 22: "And without shedding of blood is no remission." I would like to ask those men who do not believe in the blood, What are you going to do with your sins? Would you insult the Almighty by offering Him the fruit of your body to atone for them? Can a *man* atone for sin? If there is a scoffer here, a man who makes light of the blood, I want to know what he is going to do?

A gentleman once came to me and said, "If you are right, I am wrong; and if I am right, you are wrong."

I saw he was a minister, and I said, "Well, I never heard you preach; if you have heard me you can tell what the difference is. Where do we differ?"

"Well, you preach the death of Christ; I preach His life. I tell people His death has nothing to do with their salvation; you tell them His life has nothing to do with it, and that His death only will save them. I do not believe a word of it."

"Well," I said, "what do you do with this passage, 'Who His own self bare our sins in His own body on the tree'?"

"Well, I have never preached on that text."

"What do you do with this, then, 'Ye are not redeemed with corruptible things as silver and gold, but with the precious blood of Christ'?"

"I have never preached on that text either," was the reply.

"Well, what do you do with this, 'Without shedding of blood there is no remission'?"

"I have never spoken on that," he said.

"What do you do with this, 'He was wounded for our transgressions, He was bruised for our iniquities, the chastisement of our peace was upon Him'?"

"I have never preached on that either."

"What *do* you preach, then?" I asked.

He hesitated for a little, and then said, "I preach moral essays."

"You leave out the atonement?"

"Yes."

"Well," I said, "it would all be a sham to me if I did that; I could not understand it. I would be away home to-morrow, I would not know what to preach. Moral essays on Christ without His death!"

The young man said, "Well, it does seem a sham sometimes."

He was honest enough to confess that. Why, the whole thing is a myth without the atonement. The crucifixion of Christ is the foundation of the whole matter. If a man is unsound on the blood, he is unsound in everything. "Without shedding of blood is no remission."

Turn now to Hebrews x. 11. Hebrews is full of the blood. "And every priest standeth daily ministering and offering oftentimes the same sacrifices, which can never take away sins. But this Man"—what Man? the Man Christ Jesus—"after He had offered one sacrifice for sins, forever sat down on the right hand of God." One sacrifice for sins forever! He has offered as a sacrifice *Himself*. You need no lambs now, no bullocks now. The High Priest has offered Himself. The high priest of old could not take his seat; his work was never done. But our great High Priest went up on high, and took His seat on the right hand of the Father's throne; the work is done. "It is finished," He said. All the types and shadows are fulfilled in Him, and now they have vanished away.

I believe if a man could get to heaven without the blood of Christ, he would not be happy there. He could not join in the great song that is sung around the throne; he could not sing the song of Moses and the Lamb; he could not say he was redeemed by the blood of the Lamb. You would see him away in some corner, out of tune with the rest; he would not be in harmony with them, and would not wish to stay there. But he could not get there. The only way is by the new and living way that Christ opened.

Turn back again to Hebrews x. 19: "Having, therefore, brethren, boldness to enter into the holiest by the blood of Jesus, by a new and living way which He hath consecrated for us, through the veil, that is to say, His flesh." Those Jews, before Christ died, had to have the high priest intercede for them. He used to go in once a year into the holy of holies with blood to make intercession; but since Christ, our great High Priest, came, we do not need any Aaron to intercede for us. When Christ died, He opened a new and living way. He made us all kings and priests. It is said that the veil that was rent was His flesh. When He cried on the cross, "It is finished," the veil of the temple was rent in twain. God seized it with His right hand and tore it away. No veil between God and man now! We need no one to intercede for us now. Christ has died, yea, is risen again. Yes, we are all kings and priests now; we can go straight to the holy of holies ourselves. We need no man to intercede for our souls. The moment a man is saved by the blood he becomes a king and a priest. God calls him "My son." He is an heir of heaven and of glory. He is redeemed by the blood; he is made nigh by the blood. He gets victory over the world, the flesh, and the devil, by the blood.

There is a very solemn verse in Hebrews x. 28. "He that despised Moses' law died without mercy under two or three witnesses; of how much sorer punishment, suppose ye, shall he be thought worthy, who hath trodden under foot the Son of God, and hath counted the blood of the covenant wherewith he was sanctified an unholy thing, and hath done despite unto the Spirit of grace?" If a man despised Moses' law, they led him out and stoned him to death. Sinner, let me ask you, What are you going to do with the blood of God's only Son? I tell you it is a terrible thing to make light of the blood, to laugh and ridicule the doctrine of the blood. I would rather fall dead on this platform than do such a thing. It makes my heart shudder when I hear men speak lightly of it.

Some time ago a very solemn thought came stealing over me, and made a deep impression on my mind. The only thing that Christ left of His body on the earth was His blood. His flesh and bones He took away, but when He went up on high, He left His blood down here. What are you going to do with the blood? Are you going to make light of it and trample on it? May God give us all a glimpse of Christ crucified!

Revelation is full of the doctrine of the blood. "They overcame by the blood of the Lamb and the word of their testimony." That is the only way to overcome the devil, the lion of hell—by the blood of the Lamb. He knows that the moment a poor sinner flees to the blood he is beyond his reach.

As I have traveled up and down Christendom I have found out that a minister who gives a clear sound upon this doctrine is successful. A man who covers up the Cross, though he may be an intellectual man, and draw large crowds, will have no life there, and his church will be but a gilded sepulchre. Those who preach the doctrine of the Cross, and hold up Christ as the sinner's only hope of heaven, and as the sinner's only substitute, who make much of the blood, God honors. Souls are always saved in the church where the blood of Christ is preached.

May God help us to make much of the blood of His Son. It cost God so much to give us His Son, and shall we try to keep Him from the world which is perishing from the want of Him? The world can get along without us, but not without Christ. Let us preach Christ in season and out of season. Let us go to the sick and dying, and hold up the Savior who came to seek and save them—who died to redeem them. "They overcame by the blood of the Lamb and the word of their testimony."

Once more, in Revelation vii. 14. "These are they which came out of great tribulation, and have washed their robes and made them white in the blood of the Lamb." Sinner, how are you going to get your robes clean if you do not get them washed in the blood of the Lamb? How are you going to wash them? Can you make them clean?

I pray that at last we may all get back to the paradise above. There they are singing the sweet song of redemption. May it be the happy lot of each of us to

join them. It will be a few years at the longest before
we shall be there to sing the sweet song of Moses and
the Lamb. But if you die without Christ, without hope,
and without God, where will you be? O sinner, be
wise; do not make light of the blood. An aged minister
of the Gospel, on his dying bed, said:

"Bring me the Bible."

Putting his finger upon the verse, "The blood of Jesus
Christ His Son cleanseth us from all sin," he said. "I
die in the hope of this verse."

It was not his fifty years' preaching, but the blood of
Christ. May God grant that when we come at last to
stand before the great white throne, our robes may be
washed in the cleansing blood of Christ!

"WHAT THINK YOU OF THE CROSS?"

By RIGHT REV. J. C. RYLE, Bishop of Liverpool

What do you think and feel about the Cross of Christ?
You live in a Christian land. You probably attend the
worship of a Christian church. You have perhaps been
baptized in the name of Christ. You profess and call
yourself a Christian. All this is well—it is more than
can be said of millions in the world; but it is no answer
to my question. *"What do you think about the Cross
of Christ?"*

I want to tell you what the greatest Christian perhaps
that ever lived thought about the Cross of Christ. He
has written down his opinion in the letter which the
Holy Ghost inspired him to write to the Galatians; and
the words in which his judgment is set down, are these:

"God forbid that I should glory, save in the Cross of
our Lord Jesus Christ."

Reader, let me talk to you about this subject. It is
one of the deepest importance. This is no mere question
of controversy. This is not one of those points on
which men may agree to differ, and feel that differences
will not shut them out of heaven. A man must be
right on this subject, or he is lost forever. Heaven or
hell, happiness or misery, life or death, blessing or
cursing in the last day—all hinges on the answer to
this question, "What do you think about the Cross of
Christ?"

There are many things that Paul might have gloried in, if he had thought as some do in this day. If there was ever one on earth who had something to boast of in himself, that man was the great apostle of the Gentiles. Now if he did not dare to glory, who shall?

He never glorified in *his national privileges*. He was a Jew by birth, and as he tells us himself—"An Hebrew of the Hebrews." He might have said, like many of his brethren, "I have Abraham for my forefather. I am not a dark, unenlightened heathen. I am one of the favored people of God. I have been admitted into covenant with God by circumcision. I am a far better man than the ignorant Gentiles." But he never glorified in anything of this kind, never for one moment!

He never glorified in *his own works*. None ever worked so hard for God as he did. He was more abundant in labors than any of the apostles. No living man ever preached so much, travelled so much, and endured so many hardships for Christ's cause. None ever converted so many souls, did so much good in the world, and made himself so useful to mankind. No father of the early church, no reformer, no Puritan, no missionary, no minister, no layman—no one man could ever be named, who did so many good works as the apostle Paul.

But did he ever glory in them, as if they were in the least meritorious, and could save his soul?

Never! never for one moment!

He never gloried in *his own knowledge*. He was a man of great gifts naturally, and after he was converted the Holy Spirit gave him greater gifts still. He was a mighty preacher, and a mighty speaker, and a mighty writer. He was as great with his pen as he was with his tongue. He could reason equally well with Jews and Gentiles. He could argue with infidels at Corinth, or Pharisees at Jerusalem, or self-righteous people in Galatia. He knew many deep things. He had been in the third heaven, and heard unspeakable words. He had received the spirit of prophecy, and could foretell things yet to come.

But did he ever glory in his knowledge, as if it could justify him before God?

Never! never for one moment!

He never gloried in *his graces*. If ever there was one who abounded in graces, that man was Paul. He was full of love. How tenderly and affectionately he used to write! He could feel for souls like a mother or a nurse feeling for her child. He was a bold man—he cared not what risks he ran when souls were to be won. He was a self-denying man—in hunger and thirst often, in cold and nakedness, in watchings and fastings. He was a humble man—he thought himself less than the least of all saints, and the chief of sinners. He was a prayerful man—see how it comes out at the beginning of all his epistles. He was a thankful man—his thanksgivings and his prayers walked side by side. But he never gloried in all this, never rested his soul's hopes on it. Oh! no! never for a moment!

He never gloried in *his churchmanship*. If ever there was a good churchman, that man was Paul. He was himself a chosen apostle, a founder of churches, and an ordainer of ministers. He was the beginner of services and sacraments in many a dark place. Many a one did he baptize, many a one did he receive to the Lord's table.

But did he ever glory in his office and church

standing? Does he ever speak as if his churchmanship would save him, justify him, put away his sins, and make him acceptable before God?

Oh! no! never for a moment!

And now, mark what I say. If the apostle Paul never glorified in any of these things, who in all the world has any right to glory in them in our day? If Paul said, "God forbid that I should glory in anything whatever except the Cross," who shall dare to say, "I have something to glory of—I am a better man than Paul?"

The Cross means that Christ died for sinners upon the cross, that He made atonement for sinners by His suffering for them on the cross—a complete and perfect sacrifice for sin which He offered up, when He gave His own body to be crucified. This is the meaning in which Paul used the expression, when he told the Corinthians, "The preaching of the Cross is to them that perish foolishness" (1 Cor. i. 18), and when he wrote to the Galatians, "God forbid that I should glory save in the Cross," he simply meant, "I glory in nothing but Christ crucified, as the salvation of my soul."

This is the subject *he loved to preach about*.

He was a man who went to and fro on the earth, proclaiming to sinners that the son of God had shed His own heart's blood to save their souls, that Jesus Christ had loved them, and died for their sins upon the cross. Mark how he says to the Corinthians, "I delivered unto you first of all that which I also received, how that Christ died for our sins" (1st Cor. ii: 2). He—a blaspheming, persecuting Pharisee—had been washed in Christ's blood. He could not hold his peace about it. He was never weary of telling the story of the Cross.

This is the subject *he loved to dwell upon when he wrote* to believers.

It is wonderful to observe how full his epistles generally are of the sufferings and death of Christ. He enlarges on the subject constantly. He returns to it continually. It is the golden thread that runs through all his doctrinal teaching and practical exhortation. He seems to think that the most advanced Christian can never hear too much of the Cross.

This is what *he lived upon* all his life, from the time of his conversion. He tells the Galatians, "The life that I now live in the flesh I live by the faith of the Son of God, who loved me and gave Himself for me" (Gal. ii: 20). What made him so strong to labor, so willing to work, so unwearied in endeavoring to save some, so persevering and patient? The secret of it all was that he was always feeding by faith on Christ's body and Christ's blood. Jesus crucified was the meat and drink of his soul.

And, reader, you may rest assured that Paul was right. The Cross of Christ—the death of Christ on the cross to make atonement for sinners—is the central truth in the whole Bible. This is the truth we begin with when we open Genesis. The seed of the woman bruising the serpent's head is nothing else but a prophecy of Christ crucified. This is the truth that shines out, though veiled, all through the law of Moses and the history of the Jews. The daily sacrifice, the Passover lamb, the continual shedding of blood in the tabernacle and temple—all these were emblems of Christ crucified. This is the truth that we see honored in the vision of heaven before we close the book of Revelation. "In the midst of the throne and of the four beasts," we are told, "and in the midst of the elders, stood a Lamb as it had been slain'' (Rev. v: 6). Even in the midst of heavenly glory we get a view of Christ crucified. Take away the Cross of Christ, and the Bible is a dark book. It is like the Egyptian hieroglyphics without the key that interprets their meaning, curious and wonderful, but of no real use.

Reader, mark what I say. You may know a good deal about the Bible. You may know the outlines of the histories it contains, and the dates of the events described, just as a man knows the history of England. You may know the names of the men and women mentioned in it, just as a man knows Caesar, Alexander the Great, or Napoleon. You may know the several precepts of the Bible, and admire them, just as a man admires Plato, Aristotle, or Seneca. But if you have not yet found out that Christ crucified is the foundation of the whole volume, you have read your Bible hitherto to very little profit. Your religion is a heaven without a sun, an arch without a keystone, a compass without a needle, a clock without spring or weights, a lamp without oil. It will not comfort you. It will not deliver your soul from hell.

You may know a great deal about Christ by a kind of head knowledge. You may know who He was, and where He was born, and what He did; his miracles, His sayings, His prophecies, and His ordinances; how He lived, how He suffered, and how He died. But unless you know the power of Christ's Cross by experience —unless you know and feel within that the blood shed on that cross has washed away your own particular sins —unless you are willing to confess that your salvation depends entirely upon the work that Christ did upon the cross—Christ will profit you nothing. The mere knowing Christ's name will never save you. You must know His Cross and His blood, or else you will die in your sins.

Beware of a religion in which there is not much of the Cross. You live in times when the warning is sadly needful. Beware, I say again, of a religion without the Cross.

There are hundreds of places of worship in this day, in which there is everything almost except the Cross. There is carved oak, and sculptured stone. There is stained glass, and brilliant paintings. There are solemn services, and a constant round of ordinances. But the real Cross of Christ is not there. Jesus crucified is not proclaimed in the pulpit. The Lamb of God is not lifted up, and salvation by faith in Him is not freely proclaimed. Hence all is wrong. Reader, beware of such places of worship. They are not *apostolical;* they would not have satisfied St. Paul.

There are thousands of religious books published in our times, in which there is everything except the Cross. They are full of directions about sacraments, and praises of the church. They abound in exhortations about holy living, and rules for the attainment of perfection. But the real Cross of Christ is left out. The Savior and His dying love are either not mentioned. or mentioned in an unscriptural way. Hence they are worse than useless. Reader, beware of such books. They are not *apostolical*. They would never have satisfied St. Paul.

I think it is an excellent thing for us all to be continually dwelling on the Cross of Christ. It is a good thing to be often reminded how Jesus was betrayed into

the hands of wicked men, how they condemned Him
with most unjust judgment, how they spit on Him,
scourged Him, beat Him, and crowned Him with thorns;
how they led Him as a lamb to the slaughter, without
His murmuring or resisting; how they drove the nails
through His hands and feet, and set Him up on Calvary
between two thieves; how they pierced His side with a
spear, mocked Him in His sufferings, and let Him hang
there naked and bleeding until He died. Of all these
things, I say, it is good to be reminded.

It is not for nothing that the crucifixion is described
four times over in the New Testament. There are very
few things that all the four writers of the Gospel describe. Generally speaking, if Matthew, Mark, and
Luke tell a thing in our Lord's history, John does not
tell it. But there is one thing that all the four give
us most fully, and that one thing is the story of the
Cross.

This is a telling fact, and not to be overlooked.

People seem to me to forget that all Christ's sufferings on the cross were *necessary for man's salvation.*
He had to bear our sins if ever they were to be borne at
all. With His stripes alone could we be healed. This
was the one payment of our debt that God would accept.
This was the great sacrifice on which our eternal life
depended. If Christ had not gone to the cross and
suffered in our stead, the Just for the unjust, there
would not have been a spark of hope for us. There
would have been a mighty gulf between ourselves and
God, which no man ever could have passed.

People seem to me to forget that all Christ's sufferings were endured *voluntarily* and of His own free will.
He was under no compulsion. Of His own choice He

went to the cross to finish the work He came to do. He might easily have summoned legions of angels with a word, and scattered Herod and Pilate and all their armies, like chaff before the wind. But He was a willing sufferer. His heart was set on the salvation of sinners. He was resolved to open a fountain for all sin and uncleanness, by shedding His own blood.

Reader, when I think of all this, I see nothing painful or disagreeable in the subject of Christ's Cross. On the contrary, I see in it wisdom and power, peace and hope, joy and gladness, comfort and consolation. The more I keep the Cross in my mind's eye, the more fulness I seem to discern in it. The more I am satisfied that there is more to be learned at the foot of the cross than anywhere else in the world.

The Cross is *the strength of a minister.* I for one would not be without it for all the world. I should feel like a soldier without arms, like an artist without his pencil, like a pilot without his compass, like a laborer without his tools. Let others, if they will, preach the law and morality. Let others hold forth the terrors of hell and the joys of heaven. Give me the Cross of Christ. This is the only lever which has ever turned the world upside down hitherto, and made men forsake their sins.

And if this will not, nothing will. A man may preach with a perfect knowledge of Latin, Greek, and Hebrew, but he will do little or no good among his hearers unless he knows something of the Cross. Never was there a minister who did much for the conversion of souls who did not dwell much on Christ crucified. Luther, Rutherford, Whitfield, M'Cheyne were all most eminently preachers of the Cross. This is the preaching that the

Holy Ghost delights to bless. He loves to honor those who honor the Cross.

The Cross is *the secret of all missionary success*. Nothing but this has ever moved the hearts of heathen. Just according as this has been lifted up missions have prospered. This is the weapon that has won victories over hearts of every kind, in every quarter of the globe. Greenlanders, Africans, South-Sea Islanders, Hindoos, Chinese, all have alike felt its power. Just as a huge iron bridge is more affected and bent by half an hour's sunshine than by all the dead weight that can be placed in it, so in like manner the hearts of savages have melted before the Cross when every other argument seemed to move them no more than stones.

"Brethren," said a North American Indian after his conversion, "I have been a heathen and know how heathens think. Once a preacher came and began to explain to us that there was a God; but we told him to return to the place from whence he came. Another preacher came and told us not to lie, or steal, or drink; but we did not heed him. At last another came into my hut one day and said, 'I have come to you in the name of the Lord of heaven and earth. He sends to let you know that He will make you happy, and deliver you from misery. For this end He became a man, gave His life a ransom, His blood for sinners.' I could not forget his words. I told them to the other Indians, and an awakening begun among us."

I say, therefore, reach the sufferings and death of Christ our Savior if you wish your words to gain entrance among the heathen.

The Cross is *the foundation of a church's prosperity*. No church will ever be honored in which Christ crucified is not continually lifted up. Nothing whatever can make up for the want of the Cross. Without it all things may be done decently and in order. Without it there may be splendid ceremonies, beautiful music, learned ministers, crowded communion tables, large collections for the poor; but without the Cross no good will be done. Dark hearts will not be enlightened, proud hearts will not be humbled, mourning hearts will not be comforted, fainting hearts will not be cheered. A gorgeous banqueting room and splendid gold plate on the table will never make up to a hungry man for the want of food. Christ crucified is God's grand ordinance for doing good to men. Whenever a church keeps back Christ crucified, or puts anything whatever in that foremost place which Christ crucified should always have, from that moment the church ceases to be useful.

Without Christ crucified in her pulpits, a church is little better than a cumberer of the ground, a dead carcass, a well without water, a barren fig tree, a sleeping watchman, a silent trumpet, a dumb witness, an embassador without terms of peace, a messenger without tidings, a light-house without fire, a stumbling-block to weak believers, a comfort to infidels, a hot-bed for formalism, a joy to the devil, and an offence to God.

THE SPRINKLED BLOOD

By REV. W. HAY H. M. AITKEN

"And ye shall take a bunch of hyssop, and dip it in the blood that is in the bason, and strike the lintel and the two side posts with the blood that is in the bason; and none of you shall go out at the door of his house until the morning. For the Lord will pass through to smite the Egyptians; and when He seeth the blood upon the lintel, and on the two side posts, the Lord will pass over the door, and will not suffer the destroyer to come into your houses to smite you" (Ex. xii. 22, 23).

Our text leads us to the consideration of an episode which must be regarded as altogether unique in sacred history.

It was "a night much to be remembered," that strange night in which the Lord "passed over the land of Egypt." It was a night which has been much remembered. Wherever the Bible has gone, the story of that night has passed with it. Wherever a Jew exists on the face of God's earth, it is to this night he points as the proudest epoch in his national history. Yes, although at that moment they were but a nation of slaves, there is something in this incident which distinguished it from all historical incidents. It stands alone as an instance of Divine intervention, direct and unmistakable, by which a nation of slaves was suddenly exalted, lifted up from a state of serfdom; the staff of the oppressor, the rod of Pharaoh, broken as by the arm of Omnipotence; and they themselves exalted to be a nation of priests unto their Father in heaven.

You and I who live in the sunlight of God's revealed love in Christ, are able to look back upon the record of that night, and discover in it a most striking and marvelously complete illustration of the glorious work which was performed upon the Cross of Calvary.

There are three great truths to which our minds are directed.

CONDEMNATION

The first point is the doctrine of the *universality of condemnation*. God is going to save the Israelites; yes, but before He saves them He will condemn them. God is going to smite the Egyptians; but before He does so, God shall make it plain to all intelligences that He is "no respector of persons," that in His sight "all have sinned" and therefore all have deserved punishment.

How does He do it?

He sends Moses with a message couched in the language of symbol, which said clearly to those who had spiritual discernment:

"You Israelites, like your oppressors, are all guilty. Your actual state before God (notwithstanding your covenant privileges) is one of guilt. The result of that guilt is that you have brought yourself under punishment. The bondage of Egypt is the legitimate consequence of your own national guilt; but I am coming to deliver you from that bondage, and, ere I do that, I must bring you in guilty, and show you to yourselves in the true light of Divine justice. Take you a lamb. I can not pass your house until I have first of all shown you what your sins merit. I am going to visit the Egyptians yonder, but I am also going to visit you. I am going to let death do its work in yonder habitations;

death shall do its work in yours, too. Before I can deliver you from the state to which your sins have reduced you, I must first of all put you in your true position, and that is one of actual condemnation in My sight. I cannot pass over you until first of all you have been convicted.''

The sentence of death goes forth. The message is sent direct from God. Every Israelite is to ''take a lamb,'' and that lamb is to be regarded as the representative of the first-born of the house, and the first-born of the house is to be regarded as the representative of the family.

Let us endeavor to impress this truth upon ourselves, the truth continually forced upon our understanding in New Testament Scriptures, ''All have sinned, and come short of the glory of God.''

And what is the result of all having sinned?

Unquestionably that we are all under condemnation.

There are some people who seem to think that if they can only extenuate their sins, and show that they are not as great as their neighbor's, they will be in a position to hold up their heads with confidence before Almighty God; but I want to point out to you that God's sentence has gone forth: ''The soul *that sinneth*''—not the soul that sinneth *much,* or the soul that sinneth *little*—but ''the soul that sinneth, *it shall die.*'' And to every man and woman in this world the sentence of God's justice is the same. ''O, wicked man''—whether thy sins are outward, or whether they are merely the sins of the heart, which the eye of man has never seen, but which lie patent before the eye of the Almighty—''O wicked man, thou shalt surely die!'' That is God's sentence against sin.

THE FIRST SIN

Do you ask what God means by the sentence? I take you back to the first occasion on which it was carried into execution.

When was that?

At the moment when Adam disobeyed God.

Was Adam damned the moment he sinned?

No; but he died. "In the day that thou eatest thereof, thou shalt surely die." Death entered into him the very moment that he sinned against God.

What was this death?

He did not drop down then and there in the Divine presence; he was not suddenly paralyzed by the arrest of "that stern sergeant, death." No, he lived hundreds of years afterwards. But he was "dead" at that moment.

What was that death?

When he was created, "God breathed into his nostrils the breath of life." There came into man's nature a power that emanated from God Himself, and bound him to its source. But the moment that that first created man sinned, that moment the blessed connecting link between God, the Author of life, and man, the recipient of life, was severed, and the result was death.

A PARABLE FROM NATURE

Go to that splendid, stately oak. Look at one of its branches, full of life and vigor, putting forth its leaves in all its verdure. Where does it get its life from? It gets its life from the trunk. Suppose you draw a saw across that branch and sever it from the trunk, it remains green still. The leaves do not suddenly wither;

there is no particular external difference in its appearance. Yet is there a difference? What is it? It is here. In the one case it is alive, in the other it is practically dead. All the botanists in the world cannot make it live. So it is with the human soul. The keen edge of sin slips in between God, who is the source of life, and man, who is its recipient. Take away the breath of the Most High, and the connection between me and my God ceases that moment. Dying, we die! Look at the branch, it is not dead, and yet it is dead; though in another sense it is dying. You pass it day by day, and you see the green leaves gradually searing; the lithesome branches becoming more and more brittle. Let a few months pass over it, and its leaves will be rotten and its wood be dry. Its death has been perfected; but it began the moment that the branch was severed from the trunk.

In that branch we may learn the mystery of spiritual death. Wherever sin is, it cuts me off from God; and therefore if there are any here who do not think themselves great sinners, I would say to them, Your sin may have been a very thin and keen-edged tool, but it has done its work. It has severed between you and your God. That is all, but it is enough; and therefore "you are dead in trespasses and sins." In God's sight the fatal issue is already preconceived. God already sees you lost. Hell differs from the sinner's life on earth in degree, and not in kind. Hell is eternal death; but it is only the final development of a death which has begun already.

Now, dear friends, that is not a very comforting consideration for you, is it? We don't envy the case of the man upon whom sentence of death has been pronounced, and who is waiting in the condemned cell for his execution! Go to your balls, go to your theatres, buy your property, deck your houses, bedizen your body, rush into all sorts of worldly excitements, and all the while just repeat to yourself:

"I am a sinner, under sentence of death—condemned, *condemned*, CONDEMNED ALREADY!"

It is not the preacher who says that. It is a greater than any mere man. The voice of Eternal Truth hath said it—"He that believeth not is condemned already." There is no necessity to wait for the judgment day.

O men and women, there are some of you who know, alas, how well! that the brand of God's condemnation was upon your brow. And yet you sit quietly, unconcernedly in your seat now—a condemned soul. Devils know it, and exult in it. Angels know it, and mourn over it. God knows it. Your own conscience knows it. And the sooner you confess it to God, and make common cause with Him in this matter, the better for yourselves.

SUBSTITUTION

The second great lesson we see in this remarkable incident is the lesson of *substitution*. God's will was that on this occasion He should show forth the "exceeding greatness of His love to us-ward who believe"—His favor towards His own people.

And how does He do it?

He sends Moses on an errand to His favored ones, and tells them to "choose a lamb, for every family a lamb." The lamb was to be chosen as *the representative of the first-born*, just as the first-born was the representative of the family.

We can imagine the scene. The shadows of evening are closing in; the paschal night is drawing near. There is the little innocent lamb, pure and spotless— "without blemish." There it stands, a guiltless creature! It has done no harm. There is no sin in that poor animal. Side by side with that lamb there stands the first-born son, the representative of the guilt of the family. He is a sinner himself; his brothers and sisters are all sinners; and the accumulated guilt of the family meets on that first-born's head. There he is, guilty before God; the curse resting upon him, and upon him it would have rested, but for that innocent lamb at his side. The shadows of evening are closing, the sacrificial act has to be performed. Another moment, and the lamb is lying prostrate in its blood on the earth. Poor innocent victim, there it lies, bleeding, dying; and the first-born son sees in that outpoured blood his forfeited life. "That lamb represents what was due against me; the penalty due to me is exacted from that innocent victim, and because the lamb has died, therefore I may go free."

So the substitution has been affected by each family in the land of Goshen. And now we will turn from thence to Calvary.

It is a more interesting sight that meets us than that in the humble home of the Israelite in the land of Egypt. Behold the dying Lamb of God! There He hangs with the world's guilt upon Him, representing and bearing in His own Person the entire sin of humanity from the first disobedience till the stroke of doom, when a guilty world, smitten with God's vengeance, shall roll down to the doom that it has deserved.

There He hangs—His head is bowed, His heart is breaking. All around Him there is darkness.

What means that wild, that melancholy cry? that cry of agony wrung from an excruciated, from a breaking heart, what means it—"My God! My God! why hast thou forsaken Me?"

Surely it means that the Son of God has become the representative of man. The Lamb of God has become the sin-bearer. The keen edge of the sword of death hath severed the pure and holy representative of a world's guilt from the life and the joy and the blessedness of conscious communion with His Father. Sin hath done its baleful work; sin, reaching out its deadly hand, has couched that innocent soul.

There He hangs, in solitude and in darkness. The light which had followed Him in all His pilgrimage— the light which had beamed forth fresh and rull into His human nature, filling Him with the very jubilee of heaven, making the shadows of earth flee, that light of His Father's favor is eclipsed. He, the eternal Prince of Life, becomes subject to the malignant power of death, nothing less than that!

Now, our eyes are open, and we gaze upon the scene with, oh what interest! Side by side with the Lamb of God we see—not a first-born son—not one solitary boy —but the whole human family. Oh, let us in thought gather with tens of millions of our race round the Cross. We watch every feature of that agonized face, with the inward consciousness that, upon the dying suffering of that bleeding Lamb, our own eternal interests are depending, and that if His firm will yield—if His heart give way—if, under the supernatural, hellish pressure the love of Jesus for one moment fails—if, lifting up those dying, languid eyes, He should plead with the Father for ten legions of angels to deliver Him from the anguish of His despair—if He blench, or flinch, or hesitate, or give place to a single thought that shall be out of harmony with the Divine purpose, that very moment our future is decided: we are lost, we perish forever! But glory to Him! He did not blench, and He did not quail. "He trod the wine-press alone; and of the people there was none with Him."

There He hung, all alone, while the three hours crept on their tardy course. Then there comes a voice of triumph—even from out the very depths of nature's despair, He cries, "It is finished!" and in another moment the smile of peace is resting on His dying features. "Father!" He says, "into Thy hands I commend My spirit": and "when He had said this, He gave up the ghost."

GOD SATISFIED

God saw it and God was satisfied. Do you doubt that God was satisfied? Look at yonder broken tomb, and read there God's vindication of the finished work of His Son.

Answer this question. Who was it He represented when He went under the shadow of death? Was it Himself or was it men?

If He represented the whole family in His death, then surely He did not cease to represent the whole family when that death had come to its end? He represents man still in that glorious moment when the Lord God Omnipotent, by His own resistless power, bursts the barriers of the grave, snaps the bars of death, and lifts His only begotten to His own right hand

There and then God manifested to every disquieted conscience, and to every troubled heart, that the satisfaction has not only been offered, but has been accepted, inasmuch as He was our Substitute. If there had been one sin with respect to which God was not satisfied, one single point of human guilt that had not been fully expiated, the blessed and immaculate Substitute of the human family must of necessity have continued to represent human sin under the shadows of death and separation from His God until such time as the expiation was accomplished. But because the expiation was complete, no sooner has the sentence of death been borne than God manifests to all intelligence how thoroughly satisfied He is with what His Son has done. Then He lifts Him from the shadows of death. The penalty hath been borne, and man may now be free!

APPROPRIATION

Now if we have got those two points into our minds, we will go on to the third.

Say some, If Jesus Christ really died for all, then all must be forgiven. By no means. There is something else to be considered besides satisfaction.

We will go back again into the court of that oriental home. There the family are gathered together, the lamb is slain, the blood is lying there in the basin.

What about the first-born son?

His heart may beat more lightly now, if he had any knowledge of his danger; he may have realized, "There is a substitution found for me. That bleeding lamb my God has ordained to represent my guilt, and he has died."

Yes; but was the first-born out of danger?

He was as much in danger as ever he had been before!
Nay, further, I venture to think he was even more in
danger; for not only was he still a sinner, but until
God's further command had been obeyed, he was a
disobedient sinner; he was a sinner who had failed to
avail himself of the provisions of divine mercy. Therefore he was a sinner doubly condemned.

Dear friends, what remained to be done? Moses gave
a very clear direction. You will find it in the words of
our text. The Israelite was to take a bunch of hyssop,
he was to dip it in the blood that was in the basin, and
to sprinkle this blood upon the lintel, and upon the two
side-posts. Now, as we have considered universal *condemnation* and *substitution,* so we will go on to consider
appropriation.

Everybody knows what it is to *appropriate* a thing.
Suppose I purchase in one of your stores a costly diamond ring, and pay down the price and direct it to be
delivered to the person who comes to claim it, on his
presenting my card. To whom then does that diamond
belong? Does it belong to the storekeeper? No, because he has been paid for it. Does it belong to the
man who bought it, and paid the money for it? No,
because he has bought it for somebody else. Does it
belong to the person for whom it was bought? No, because he has not claimed it. Whom does it belong to?
The obvious answer is, it morally and really belongs to
the person for whom it was bought; legally, it belongs
to the person who bought it, and paid for it; actually
it belongs to the storekeeper, who has it still in his pos
session.

THE GIFT OF GOD

Now let us apply this illustration to the subject before us. Contemplate this "gift of God, which is eternal life," this free, glorious, blessed salvation. I ask, To whom does it belong?

Well, the Lord Jesus bought it; He did not pay silver or gold for it, but His own life. "Greater love hath no man than this, that a man lay down his life for his friends." "But God commendeth His love toward us, in that, *while we were yet sinners,* Christ died for the ungodly." Very good; it belongs then, legally to the Lord Jesus Christ. "Salvation belongeth to the Lord." It is His purchase.

Well, but for whom did He buy it? Dwelling for all eternity, in the glory of His Father, He did not want it for Himself. Salvation is not needed by Him. Whom is it bought for, then?

It was bought for you and me, my dear fellow-sinner. It is ours by His purchase.

Well, but where is this life to be found? How are we to get it?

I turn my gaze towards its eternal source, the loving, life-giving God; and I am privileged to know that the life I need is there for me. God has acknowledged the work of His Son, and recognized His claim on behalf of man; and now His eternal Spirit holds that life for us ready to convey it to our souls in all the riches of its boundless wealth.

To whom does it belong? It belongs to the Lord Jesus Christ legally, and by right, because He hath bought it. To whom does it belong? It belongs to God, the life-giving Spirit, because it is in His possession to be communicated to us. But to whom does it

belong? It belongs morally to you and me, because it
has been bought FOR US by Jesus, and it is only held by
the Holy Spirit in order that He may communicate it
to our hearts. If this is so, what is wanted? Appropriation—taking the thing home to our hearts.

How is it to be done?

I have already told you, that the eldest son was not
safe until the father took the bunch of hyssop and
struck the blood upon the lintel and the two side-posts.
Observe what he has to do with the blood. First of all,
he was to get a bunch of hyssop—I will speak of that in
a moment—then dip it in the blood, and do what? Up
yonder—on the lintel, he was to strike the blood. He
was to put the shed blood between him and his God, so
that when the everlasting Jehovah looked down upon
the condemned first-born, He might see between Him
and the sinner the precious blood of the slaughtered
lamb.

What more was he to do with it?

He was to dip the hyssop again into the blood, and
put the blood upon that post, and this post, so that it
might be on either side of him.

What was that to teach?

We belong to a sin-stricken world, and we are sur-
rounded by sin on every side. Society is permeated by
the essence of sin. When we become the Lord's, we
are not only severed from the wrath of God, but from
the sin of the world. We are cut off from our former
relationship, we put the blood on our right hand and on
our left to divide us from the sinful world. There we
stand, isolated by the blood from others on every side.
When the Israelite had thus separated himself from the
judgment of God, he separated himself also from the

judgment of Egypt; for these were the two things he had to escape from.

SAFE AT LAST

As soon as he had done that, and not till then, the first-born was—what?

"He had a *very good hope* that he might somehow or another escape the fearful penalty; it was *just possible* that the angel might not strike him.

If he had been *your* first-born son, would you have gone to bed very comfortable with that feeling? "There is my poor boy. I hope he won't be stricken by the destroying angel. I have *a good hope* about him. God is very merciful." Mother! would you have spent a very comfortable night under these circumstances? The Israelites did spend a very comfortable night—a triumphant night, a night of glorious anticipation; not a tear shed, not a sigh heard, not a misgiving thrilling through any heart, but a calm, holy confidence. Why was it? The moment that the blood from the hyssop was sprinkled upon the door-posts, that moment the first-born was SAFE. His mother might look on him and say, "God won't touch him now." His father might lay his hand upon his head and say, "My son, God is gracious to thee. His smile is resting on thee, and not His frown." So they took the body of the slain lamb into the house, and gathered around it, and made a feast of it. The victim which had borne their sins is now the source of their joy. They spread it on their board, and such a happy feast they had! As they feast, they rejoice to think that the dark wings of the Angel of Death, as he speeds his flight over the land of Egypt, can not brood over them. They are safe under the blood: SAFE UNDER THE BLOOD-STAINED LINTEL!

THE CARELESS FATHER

Now suppose for one moment that some of the Israelites were very careless, very thoughtless, very indifferent. There is a careless father; he is looking at the sun, which is just sinking away yonder in the west. The lamb is lying slain there—the blood in a basin.

The first-born son looks wistfully into his father's face and says:

"Father, aren't you going to sprinkle the blood?"

"Oh; I don't know about that," the father replies; "it is a mere matter of form. The lamb has been slain. Any time will do for sprinkling the blood."

The boy speaks again: "Father, if the blood is not sprinkled before midnight, your son's life will be forfeited."

Do you think the father would hesitate any longer about it—if he believed that? Can't you see him getting up in a hurry, saying:

"Oh my son; I have been far too careless about it. I never thought about it in that light. Let us not lose another moment."

He gets the bunch of hyssop, he dips it in the blood; in another moment he has sprinkled it on the two doorposts, and he says:

"Now, my boy, you are as safe as God can make you."

My friends! the sun is setting with some of you! The shadows of night are gathering around! the day of grace, how rapidly it is passing away! Some of you have had many calls. Your hearts are hard! I do not wonder at it. There is nothing that will harden a heart so much as rejection of the love of God. You have rejected it! Meanwhile, the sun is setting. A few more short moments, it may be, a few more calls, a few more sermons, a few more voices of warning, a few more gentle knocks by the hand of Jesus at the door of your heart—then the flash of the angel's sword shall be seen, and *another soul will have perished*. Lost—not because Jesus did not die, but because you did not sprinkle the blood!

Oh, my friends! just think for one moment of the agony of remembrance with which you must then reflect on that. Think of sitting down there in the darkness of despair, to brood over this tormenting thought, "The Son of the everlasting God died for me, and so there was nothing left for me to do but just to plead that blood! I had only to accept what Christ had done—that was all! God never asked me to shed a tear. He never told me to make a resolution. He never told me to breathe a prayer in order to save my soul. I was within a step of the Cross! I had but to accept the proffered boon, and I *spurned* it from me in my blind infatuation, and now I am lost forever."

THE BUNCH OF HYSSOP

What was the direction? "Take thee a bunch of hyssop." There is some uncertainty as to what plant now existing in those regions answers to the hyssop mentioned here. Most probably it was a plant which is now one of the commonest objects in the East; it may be found easily anywhere. It is a thing always at hand. You can hardly pass by a wall without seeing the hyssop springing out of some crevice in it. It was within reach of all. They had not to go and search for it. If God had told them that in some part of the land of Egypt, or the continent of Africa, there was a rare exotic, a plant of remarkable shape, and had said "Here is a description of it, but it is only to be found in a particular place; you may have a very long search before you discover it; but remember, if you don't get the right plant before the sun sets to-night, and dip it into the blood, and sprinkle the blood upon the lintel, and upon the two door-posts with it, then you know the blood will be of no use; I shall visit your house with death, just as if the lamb had never died at all"—supposing God has said such a thing, what would it have meant? It would have meant that God gave salvation with one hand, and took it away with the other. He would have been simply *mocking* the men He proposed to save.

Do you think there are many people who ever think or fancy that God acts in that way?

Plenty of people.

With what are we to sprinkle the blood?

Certainly FAITH is to be to us what the hyssop was to them—the means of applying the blood.

Now, faith is the very commonest of things in our social life; there is nothing commoner than faith. There is not a transaction upon the Exchange, or one between man and man in our domestic life, in which faith is not continually being evinced. If you were to take faith out of the world, we should have to stop our commerce, shut our stores, and, like a nation of wild beasts, fall to preying upon each other.

We are all continually exercising this faith; we are constantly living by it. Very good! Then God's direction is, Take of this common faith you are continually

using with your fellow-men, and apply with it the blood
of atonement. As you believe in your own husband
or wife, as you believe in your own man in business,
so you believe in a thousand different things every day
and every hour of your life; so, but with a more im-
plicit and unwavering confidence, take the faith which
God has given you, dip it in the hallowed blood, and
sprinkle that blood upon the lintel and upon the door-
posts.

But what is the reply to that direction on the part of
a large number of souls?

"Well, you see sir, if I only had *the right kind of
faith.*"

Ah, there it is. It is a rare exotic, and you have to
take a long journey to find it! You are not quite sure
of the description of it. Will you please to sit down and
define *what the right kind of faith is?* Some people
have been to the labor of doing something like that, and
at the end they have been just as far from the bunch of
hyssop as at the beginning.

Oh! friends, do you mean to say that the Son of God
died on that Cross in order to save us, to bring salvation just within our reach, and then, at the very moment when we are just going to take it, that He imposes
an impossible condition between us and salvation, and
we have to stand off, die and be damned, just because
we can not find the right kind of faith? Are we to
accept His Word? The Bible tells us nothing about
any special kind of faith; but it must be the same faith
of the heart which we are continually conscious of
towards our fellow men.

We very seldom allow ourselves to indulge in mere
mental faith towards other people. We believe in each

other with our hearts as well as with our minds. We trust in a man's word, we trust his honesty, not because we have an intellectual theory about it, but because in our hearts we have confidence in him. So St. Paul says, "With the heart man believeth unto righteousness." As we have faith in our fellow men, let us trust the Savior. Take a bunch of hyssop from the crack in the wall, dip it in the blood. BELIEVING is just taking the fact as a fact; TRUSTING is just reposing complete and thorough confidence in a person. Let us take these two ideas together. Let us take the fact as if it were a fact, and let us repose our full confidence in the person of Christ, and so let us claim the purchased salvation; and when that has been done, we have taken the bunch of hyssop, and sprinkled with it the blood, and from that moment let all the devils in hell condemn us, we are as *safe* in God's sight as if in heaven.

THE BLOOD

What are you going to do with "the blood"? Dip "the hyssop" in it. Let your faith be saturated with the blood, and when your faith is saturated with the blood, then put it between you and God. Yes, I speak it with reverence, it is not that God hates us, but it is that we have a double relationship to our God. As Judge, He must judge us, as surely as because He is our Father He must love us. I see His *justice* coming down to smite me; I put the blood between me and it. "Father, all Thy claims are met to the full in that blood. Now, Father, canst Thou smite me? Nay, I can stand under the blood-stained lintel, and look up with perfect confidence into the eyes of the Angel of Death, and know he must pass over me."

THE ANGEL OF DEATH

Supposing you and I had been in the land of Egypt, passing through the air with that angel. First of all we should have visited the land of Goshen—the judgment began with the people of God; it always does. Just picture it to yourselves. Here we are drawing nigh to a little humble cottage. Our eyes are strained; by the faint light of the moon we just fancy we see something in the distance. Is it what we are looking for? We get a little nearer. The archangel lays his hand on the hilt of his sword. A little nearer, and we see it there, just a tiny stain upon the lintel, another stain upon the right hand, and other stain upon the left. We look back and see a bright smile upon the dread angel's face.

"Withdraw thy sword. Thou hast no victim here!"

We look inside the little house. Happy faces are smiling there. The father is giving thanks to God, the mother is bowing her head in adoring gratitude, the children are singing hymns of praise, and there upon the table is the paschal lamb. The feast is spread, and there is the voice of triumph and of joy. Oh blessed night! It is "a night much to be remembered before the Lord."

We pass on in the company of the dark Angel of Death. Now we find ourselves halting before magnificent towers and bulwarks—a gorgeous royal palace, with a massive porch of rich marble, and splendid with carved imagery. Our eager eyes bend towards the entrance. A sentinel marches to and fro, decked in the uniform of the king's body-guard; the banners wave over the towers as the moonbeams shine out. We draw near. We look narrowly at the lintel. Is it a lichen stain, or is it blood? We look again. Ah! there is no blood there. We look at the side-posts, we scrutinize those marble columns and splendid cornices. But there is no blood there! Another moment and there is a flash of the angel's sword, and a shriek of anguish through the startled household. Lights are flitting to and fro, and in another moment the woeful tidings burst upon the land that the heir of Pharaoh's royal house is lying stark and dead, stricken by the sword of death.

And why?

Because there was *no blood*.

Is it sprinkled on you, dear friends? Who knows how near your son may be to the western horizon? The shadows may be gathering around you, and that night be drawing near in which no blood can be sprinkled. Is it sprinkled? Lo, the Angel of Death lays his hand on the hilt of his burnished sword. Is he to speed towards thy guilty soul because there is no blood there?

At a missioin I conducted some time since, I addressed a venerable looking gentleman:

"Sir, is it right with your soul?"

He said, "I should like to speak with you another time about it."

I said, "I will come and see you."

The next night I met him again. "When shall I come and see you?" I asked.

He said, "Come to-morrow, but I would like to have a word with you now." He took me aside, and said, "I must admit that I am not at peace, but I don't quite see how to obtain it. Last night, when I heard you preach, I felt a very remarkable impression; but do you know that I am a man of a very analytical turn of mind? I can not help that, for it is my natural temperament; and really what you said to-night did not commend itself to my reason as much as your last night's address did; and, as I am of an analytical turn of mind"—he paused a moment, and then burst into tears.

I saw that God was dealing with him, and merely pressed his hand and said:

"I will come and see you to-morrow, my friend."

On the morrow when I went to see him, all talk about his "analytical turn of mind" had gone. His eyes were red with weeping, and he was broken down under a sense of sin, humbled, and teachable.

I put the Gospel simply before him, "Are you content to accept it?"

He said, "O sir, I am."

We knelt down together. He received the truth like a little child; and it was not five minutes before he was pouring out his heart, praising and blessing God for what He had done for him.

That night I preached upon the sprinkled blood. When the sermon was over, and it came to the after-meeting, I saw him sitting there. He saw me passing by, lifted up his face and beckoned to me, and as I approached he took my hand in both his, and looking solemnly into my face, with tears in his eyes, he said:

"I have sprinkled the blood upon the lintel; I have sprinkled it upon the door-posts. Glory be to God!"

Can *you* say that? Will you say that? Better than saying it, will you *do* it now. "Is the blood sprinkled?"

A BLESSED PROTECTION

One word to those who have been sprinkled with blood: "Let none of you go out of your house until the morning." We cannot venture to go out from under the blood. We must live under that blessed protection. We want the blood constantly all around us, in this region of death and darkness. But when the morning dawns of the bright new day when "the Sun of Righteousness shall arise with healing in His wings," the song of triumph shall be raised, and we will come out from under the blood; and we will gaze at it, and say it was the secret of our safety. *It is* the secret of the rapture that thrills through our souls—"to Him that loved us, and washed us from our sins *in His own blood,* and hath made us kings and priests unto God and His Father; to Him be glory and dominion for ever and ever. Amen."

There were three places where the blood was to be put, and one place where the blood was *not* to be put. It was to be put up yonder, on the lintel; and there and there on the door-posts; but it was under no consideration to be put on the *doorstep,* lest men should trample it under foot. But there are men and women who have no blood upon the door-posts, no blood upon the lintel, but it is *under their feet,* trampled on with impious contempt. The blood of the covenant shed for them, the blood that preaches of the love of God; and they trample it under foot every step they take, doing despite to the Son of God that died for them, and defying the mercy that bore the pains of hell for them. Oh great God! open their eyes that they may see it; that at every breath they breathe, until they accept Thy mercy, they are trampling upon the blood of Christ!

THE RED WORD

By REV. T. DEWITT TALMAGE, D. D.

"The blood of Jesus Christ His Son cleanseth us from all sin."
1 John i. 7.

Eighteen centuries ago there lived one Jesus. Publius Lentulus, in a letter to the Roman Senate, describes Him as "a man of stature somewhat tall; His hair the color of a chestnut fully ripe, plain to the ears, whence downward it is more orient, curling and waving about the shoulders; in the midst of His forehead is a stream, or partition of His hair; forehead plain and very delicate; His face without spot or wrinkle, a lovely red; His nose and mouth so forked as nothing can be represented; His beard thick, in color like His hair—not very long; His eyes gray, quick and clear." He must die. The French army in Italy found a brass plate on which was a copy of His death warrant, signed by John Zorobabel, Raphael Robani, Daniel Robani, and Capet.

Sometimes men on the way to the scaffold have been rescued by the mob. No such attempt was made in this case, for the mob were against Him. From 9 A. M. till 3 P. M. Jesus hung a-dying. It was a scene of blood. We are so constituted that nothing is so exciting as blood. It is not the child's cry in the street that so arouses you as the crimson dripping from his lip. In the dark hall, seeing the finger-marks of blood on the plastering, you cry, "What terrible deed has been done here?" Looking upon this suspended victim of the cross, we thrill with the sight of blood—blood dripping from thorn and nail, blood rushing upon His cheek, blood saturating His garments, blood gathered in a pool beneath. There is one *red* word in the text that rouses up our attention and calls back that scene: "The BLOOD of Jesus Christ His Son cleanseth us from all sin."

ROYAL BLOOD

The blood of the Cross was *royal* blood. Through our democratic preferences, we may in theory disregard royal pretentions; yet when we see the son of a king our liveliest interest is aroused. Let the Prince of Wales go through our streets, and all the city would turn out to look.

It is called an honor to have in one's veins the blood of the house of Stuart, or of the house of Hapsburg. Is it nothing when I point you to-night to the outpouring blood of the King of the Universe?

Through the indulgences of the royal family, the physical life degenerates, and some of the kings have been almost imbecile, and their bodies weak, and their blood thin and watery; but the crimson life that flowed upon Calvary had in it the health of the immortal God.

A king dying! You remember, when the last Czar of Russia was in his fatal sickness, that bulletins were every hour dispatched from the palace, saying, "The king is better," or "The king is worse," or "The king is delirious," or "The king rested easier through the night," or "The king is dying," and "The king is dead." The bells tolled it, and flags signalled it, the telegraphs flashed it. Tell it now to all the earth and to all the heavens—Jesus our King is breathing a last groan; through His body quivers the last anguish; the King is dying; *The King is dead!*

Ye who come round about the cross, look out how you tread in what you see beneath. It is royal blood. It is said that some make too much of the humanity of Christ. I respond that we make too little. If some Roman surgeon, standing under the cross, had caught one drop of the blood on his hand and analyzed it, it would have been found to have the same plasma, the same disk, the same fibrin, the same albumen. It was unmistakably *human* blood. It is a *man* that hangs there. His bones are of the same material as ours. His nerves are sensitive like ours. If it were an angel being despoiled I would not feel it so much, for it belongs to a different order of beings. But my Savior is a *man,* and my whole sympathy is aroused. I can imagine how the spikes felt—how hot the temples burned—what deathly sickness seized His heart—how mountain and city and mob swam away from His dying vision. Something of the meaning of that cry for help makes the blood of all the ages curdle with horror, "My God! My God! why hast Thou forsaken Me?"

A BROTHER'S BLOOD

I go still farther, and say it was a *brother's* blood. If you saw an entire stranger maltreated, and his life oozing away on the pavement, you would feel indignant; but if, coming along the street, you saw a company of villains beating out the life of your own brother, the sight of his blood would make you mad. You would bound into the affray. At the peril of losing your own life you would rush in saying, "You vagabonds! this is

6

my brother, I dare you to touch him again!" You
would fight until you fell dead beside him.

That is your Brother maltreated on the Cross. They
spit on Him and slapped Him in the face. How do
you feel about that? What are your emotions as you
hear the falling of the blood upon the ground beneath—
drip, drip, drip? Do you not feel as though, with
supernatural power you could rush upon the mob? Do
you not feel as if standing close, with your back against
Him, and with one good sword in your hand, and a cry
to God for help, you could hew down the desperadoes
that assailed Him? But you cannot help. The blood
rushes from the victim, and there He hangs—your dead
Brother.

What is worse—shall I tell it?—YOU slew Him! I
charge it, first upon myself, and then upon all ye who
hear me, the awful crime of fratricide! His blood is
on our hands. Bring me a laver, quick! that I may
wash it off. Show me the pool where I may be cleansed
of the terrible stain. Here it is. I have found it. It is
the fountain opened for all sin; and though sin were
as scarlet, is shall be as snow.

SUBSTITUTION

It was *substitutionary* blood. Our sins cried to
heaven for vengeance. Some one must die. Shall it
be we or Christ?

"Let it be I," said Jesus.

You were drafted for the last war, and some one took
your place. You were in debt; not being able to meet
the obligation, some one paid it. You can easily understand how Christ went in to fight our battles and to
pay our debts The debt is cancelled; the captives are

released; the shackles are broken; the prison is opened. Blood paid the price; blood washed away the pollution; blood sealed the agreement. The blood of Paul, that soaked the dust of the guillotine, the blood of Hugh Latimer, that simmered in the fire, the blood of the high-souled martyrs, that reddened the mouths of the lions in the Coliseum, have just as much worth to your soul as the blood of Christ, unless you take this last as expiatory, and feel the truth that "the blood of Jesus Christ cleanseth from all sin."

Come, then, and get your sins pardoned! I do not ask you to come to a private confessional, or to whisper into my ears your offenses, but, where you are, to accept this moment the blood-cleansing.

First, for that old sin.

Do you ask, "What sin do you mean?"

I mean that old sin you committed years ago. It may have been two years, ten years, or twenty years. You know when it was. I think that old sins are like other debts—they increase by having the interest added on. They are tenfold greater now, and have been multiplied by all of your opportunities of having them pardoned.

Does that old sin present its dun at the door of your soul now? Can you not pay it? Does it threaten to carry you off to jail? Does it propose to sell you out? Better get together all your bonds and mortgages and certificates of stocks and United States securities. Come, let me count them!—not enough. Bring all the clever things you have ever done. Let me count them! —not enough. Bring all you possess.

You say, "I have brought everything!"

Alas! that you can not meet the obligation. you
MUST DIE!

"No! No! No!" says a voice from heaven, "The
blood of Jesus Christ, the royal blood, the human blood,
the expiatory blood, cleanseth from all sin."

"What! is that old sin gone?"

"Yes, I heard it splash into the depths of the sea. It
sinks like lead. There is no condemnation to them that
are in Christ Jesus."

Circumstances aggravate sins. If a child does wrong,
not wittingly, you excuse it; but when we do wrong,
we know it. Every time a sin is committed, conscience
tolls a funeral bell. We may laugh and pretend not to
hear it, but hear it we must. Our sins are against
warnings and reproofs, and doubly aggravated. This
man's sins are more heinous than the transgressions of
that man, because he had a better bringing up. Here
is a man who, twenty years ago, kneeled at a Methodist
altar. He went awhile on the road to heaven and then
got tired, and put off in another direction. Where he
has been since he began to backslide, he and his God
only knew. This I do know, he is wretchedly unhappy.
There is no such nest of scorpions this side of hell as
the heart of the backslider. He is the last man that
ever returns. The publicans and the harlots come in
before him. Where, oh man! is that family altar that
you once lifted? Where is the closet of prayer that
you once frequented? Are you as happy now as you
used to be? Your common sense teaches you that the
man who came to Christ, and heard the full expression
of God's love, and then went away to betray the Lord,
must drink the bitterest gall, and the thunders that at
last drive him away will roll and crash with all the

accumulated wrath of God omnipotent; and yet my text sweeps a circle of pardon around all these accumulated sins. Fire may not be able to burn them out; hoofs may not be able to trample them out; hammers may not be able to pound them out; but here is the blood that will wash them out. Come! Come!

But you say, "These things are not appropriate for me, for I am a moral man."

How about your thoughts? You see my right hand, and you see my left hand, and one as plainly as the other. So with the sin of the heart and the sin of the life—one is just as plain in God's sight as the other. You have not been guilty of murder, you say? Are you sure about that? Have you ever hated anybody? Then you are a murderer. 1 John iii:15, "Whoso hateth his brother is a murderer." You say you have never been guilty of theft. Are you sure about that? I acknowledge you have never taken anything from your fellow man; but have you not taken days and hours that belonged to God for your own purposes? If it is wrong to steal from a man, it is more wicked to rob God.

THE HOSTS OF SINS

If I could marshal before you all the sins of the best men in the world, you would shriek out with horror. Sins against God and man; sins against Sabbaths and sacraments; sins against body and soul; sins against light and knowledge; sins against Sinai and Calvary; sins against the grave and the resurrection; sins against the judgment; sins against the throne of God and the mansions of glory. I blow the trumpet, and call up all the sins of your past life, gather them into companies of hundreds; into regiments of thousands; into battalions of tens of thousands. We have a host vaster than that of Xerxes. Let the swarthiest transgression of your lifetime be general over all the host. Together let them wheel and march and fire. How the couriers of death dash up and down the line! How the great batteries of woe belch forth the sulphurous smoke of hell, and boom with the cannonading of eternal destruction! The host of thy sins innumerable, marching on to capture thy soul. One man against a million armed iniquities. Who can go forth and meet them? We must fall back and fall down. Are there no allies to help? In all the round of God's universe, is there no one to take our part?

Arise, ye seas, and whelm the host! Strike, ye lightnings, and consume the foe!

But the wave strikes the beach, and falls back crying, "No help in me!" The lightning sheathes itself in the black scabbard of the midnight cloud, and says, "No help in me!" But yonder I see a white horse in hot haste coming this way. Make room for the courier! He swings his sword. Good news! Good news! The Captain of Salvation comes to the rescue. Fall back, my sins. Fall back, my sorrows! Allies of light and love, To arms! to arms! The hosts of our sins scatter in defeat, and our delivered soul shouts, "Victory through our Lord Jesus Christ."

At the seashore you go down on the beach and into the waters, hand in hand, to bathe. None but those who have tried it know the exhilaration. I would that we might all join hands, and go down by scores, and by hundreds, and by thousands, to bathe in the great sea of God's forgiveness. Let us not stand on the margin and paddle the ripples with our feet, but plunge in until the waves go over our heads, and we come up again washed clean from all our sins. Cry mightily, that the blood of the Cross may avail for you. If it cleanse you not, it will plead against you; and all those gaping wounds of Christ, through an unknown eternity will haunt your soul with the thought of what you might have been. Oh! take your feet out of your brother's blood. Go not down condemned at last for fratricide, and regicide, and Deicide. Better for thee that Calvary had never borne its burden, and the lips of Christ had never addressed thee in invitation if, rejecting all, thou goest into eternal desolation, thy hands and feet bedabbled with the blood of the Son of God.

Oh! Ye dying but immortal men! Ye blood-bought, judgment-bound readers! Repent and believe, and hear, and live! "How shall we escape, if we neglect so great salvation?"

THE BLOOD SHED FOR MANY

By C. H. SPURGEON

The blood of Jesus has an intimate connection with remission of sins. The Bible says, "This is My blood of the new (testament) covenant, which is shed for many for the remission of sins" (Matt. xxvi: 28). Jesus, suffering, bleeding, dying, has produced for sinners the forgiveness of their sins.

Of what sins?

Of all sins of every sort and kind, however heinous, aggravated and multiplied. The blood of the covenant takes every sin away, be it what it may. There was never a sin believingly confessed and taken to Christ that ever baffled His power to cleanse it. This fountain has never been tried in vain. Murderers, thieves, liars and adulterers have come to Jesus by penitence and faith, and through the merit of His sacrifice their sins have been put away.

Of what nature is the remission?

It is pardon, freely given, acting immediately and abiding forever, so that there is no fear of the guilt ever being again laid to the charge of the forgiven one. Through the precious blood our sins are blotted out, cast into the depths of the sea, and removed as far from us as the east is from the west. Our sins cease to be. They are made an end of. They cannot be found against us any more forever. Yes, hear it, hear it, O wide earth! Let the glad news startle thy darkest dens of infamy; there is absolute remission of sins! The precious blood of Christ cleanseth from all sin; yes, turns the scarlet into a whiteness which exceeds that of the newly fallen snow—a whiteness which never can be tarnished. Washed by Jesus, the blackest sinners shall appear before the judgment-seat of the all-seeing Judge without spot.

How is it that the blood of Jesus effects this?

The secret lies in the vicarious of substitutionary character of our Lord's suffering and death. Because He stood in our place the justice of God is vindicated, and the threatening of the law is fulfilled. It is now just for God to pardon sin. Christ's bearing the penalty of human sin instead of man has made the moral government of God perfect in justice, has laid a basis for peace of conscience, and has rendered sin immeasurably hateful, though its punishment does not fall upon the believer.

This is the great secret, this is the heavenly news, the gospel of salvation, that through the blood of Jesus, sin is justly put away.

Ah, how my very soul loves this truth! Therefore do I speak it in unmistakable terms.

And for what end is this remission of sins secured?

My brethren, if there were no other end for the remission of sins but its own self, it would be a noble purpose, and it would be worth preaching every day of our lives; but it does not end here. We mistake if we think that the pardon of sins is God's ultimatum. No, no, it is but a beginning, a means to a further purpose. He forgives our sins with the design of curing our sinfulness. We are pardoned that we may become holy. God forgives the sin that He may purify the sinner.

If He had not aimed at thy holiness, there had not been so imperative a necessity for an atonement; but to impress thee with the guilt of sin, to make thee feel the evil which sin hath wrought, to let thee know thine obligation to divine love, the Lord has not forgiven thee without a sacrifice.

Ah, what a sacrifice! He aims at the death of thy sinfulness that thou mayest henceforth love Him, and serve Him, and crucify the lusts which crucified thy Lord. The Lord aims at working in thee the likeness of His dear Son. Jesus hath saved thee by His self-sacrificing obedience to justice, that thou mayest yield thy whole soul to God and be willing to die for the up-holding of the kingdom of love and truth. The death of Christ for thee pledges thee to be dead to sin, that by His resurrection from the dead thou mayest rise into newness of life, and so become like thy Lord. Pardon by blood aims at this. Dost thou catch the thought? If thou believest in the Lord Jesus Christ, God's intent is to make thee like the First-born among many brethren, and to work in thee everything that is comely and of good report.

Even this is not all. He hath a further design to bring thee into everlasting fellowship with Himself. He is sanctifying thee that thou mayest behold His face, and that thou mayest be fit to be a comrade of His only begotten Son through eternity. Thou art to be the choice and dear companion of the Lord of Love. He has a throne for thee, a mansion and a crown for thee, and an immortality of such inconceivable glory and blessedness that, if thou didst but form even a distant conception of it, no golden apple of earth would turn thee aside from pursuing the prize of thy high calling. Oh, to be forever with the Lord! Forever to behold His face!

I fail to reach the height of this great argument!
See, my brethren, to what the blood of your Lord des-
tines you. O my soul, bless God for that one cup,
which reminds thee of the great sacrifice and prophesies
to thee thy glory at the right hand of God forever!

We are told in the text that this blood is shed *"for
many* for the remission of sins." In that large word
"many" let us exceedingly rejoice. Christ's blood was
not shed for the handful of apostles alone. There were
but eleven of them who really partook of the blood
symbolized by the cup. The Savior does not say, "This
is My blood which is shed for you, the favored eleven";
but "shed for many." Jesus did not die for the ministers alone. I recollect in Martin Luther's life that
he saw, in one of the churches, a picture of the pope,
and the cardinals, and bishops, and priests, and monks,
and friars, all on board a ship. They were all safe,
everyone of them. As for the laity, poor wretches, they
were struggling in the sea, and many of them drown-
ing. Only those were saved to whom the good men in
the ship were so kind as to hand out a rope or a plank.
That is not our Lord's teaching. His blood is shed "for
many," and not for the few. He is not the Christ of a
caste, or a class, but the Christ of all conditions of
men.

Those in the upper room were all Jews, but the Lord
Jesus Christ said to them: "This blood is shed for
many," to let them see that He did not die alone for
the seed of Abraham, but for all races of men that dwell
upon the face of the earth. "Shed for many!" His
eye, I doubt not, glanced at these far-off islands, and at
the vast lands beyond the western sea. He thought of
Africa, and India, and the land of Sinim. A multitude

that no man can number gladdened the far-seeing and fore-seeing eye of the Redeemer. He spoke with joyful emphasis when He said, "shed for many for the remission of sins."

Believe in the immeasurable results of redemption. Whenever we are making arrangements for the preaching of this precious blood, let us make them on a large scale. The mansion of love should be built for a large family. The masses must be compelled to come in. A group of a half dozen converts makes us very glad, and so it should; but oh, to have half a dozen thousand at once! Why not? This blood is shed for many.

Let us cast the great net into the sea. You, young men, preach the Gospel in the streets of this crowded city, for it is meant for many! You who go from door to door, do not think you can be too hopeful, since your Savior's blood is shed for many, and Christ's "many" is a very great many. It is shed for all who ever shall believe in Him—shed for thee, sinner, if thou wilt trust Him! Only confess thy sin and trust Christ, and be assured that Jesus died in thy place and stead. It is shed for many, so that no man or woman born shall ever trust Christ in vain, or find the atonement insufficient for Him. Oh, for a large-hearted faith, so that by holy effort we may lengthen our cords, and strengthen our stakes, expecting to see the household of our Lord become exceedingly numerous!

Dwell on that word "many," and let it nerve you for far-reaching labors.

Dear reader, are you among the many? Why are you not? May His grace bring you to trust in Him, and you may not doubt that you are among the many.

"Ah," say you, "that is what I am listening for! How can I partake in the effect of this sacrifice?"

Christ is ours by our receiving Him. The merit of His precious blood becomes ours by that simple child-like faith which accepts Jesus to be our all. Christ is yours forever if you receive Him into your heart.

If thou wilt be assured that thou hast believed in Jesus, *believe again!* Whenever thou hast any doubt about whether Christ is thine, take Him over again. I like to begin again. Often I find the best way of going forward is to go back to my first faith in Jesus, and as a sinner renew my confidence in my Savior.

"Oh," says the devil, "thou art a preacher of the Gospel, but thou dost not know it thyself."

At one time I used to argue with the accuser; but he is not worth it, and it is by no means profitable to one's own heart. We cannot convert or convince the devil; it is better to refer him to our Lord. When he tells me I am not a saint, I answer:

"Well, what am I, then?"

"A sinner," says he.

"Well, so are you!"

"Ah!" saith he, "you will be lost."

"No," say I, "that is why I shall not be lost, since Jesus Christ came into the world to save sinners, and I therefore trust in Him to save me."

This is what Martin Luther called cutting the devil's head off with his own sword, and it is the best course you can follow.

I recollect a story of William Dawson, one of the best preachers that ever entered a pulpit. He once gave out his text, "Through this Man is preached unto you the forgiveness of sins." When he had given out his text he dropped down to the bottom of the pulpit, so that nothing could be seen of him, only there was a voice heard, saying:

"Not the man in the pulpit—he is out of your sight; but the Man in the Book. The Man described in the Book is the Man through whom is preached unto you the forgiveness of sins."

I put myself and you and everybody else out of sight, and I preach to you the remission of sins through Jesus only. I would sing, "Nothing but the blood of Jesus." Shut your eyes to all things but the Cross. Jesus died, and rose again, and went to heaven, and all your hope must go with Him!

Come, my reader, take Jesus by a distinct act of faith! May God the Holy Ghost constrain thee to do so, and then thou mayest go on thy way rejoicing!

THE SURETY'S CROSS

By HORATIO BONAR, D. D.

The death of the cross has always been, above every other, reckoned the death of shame. The fire, the sword, the axe, the stone, the hemlock, have in their turn been used by law as its executioners; but these have in so many cases been associated with honor that death by means of them has not been reckoned either cursed or shameful. Not so the cross. Its victim, nailed in agony to the rough wood, suspended naked and torn to the gaze of multitudes, has always been reckoned a specimen of disgrace and degraded humanity; rather to be mocked than pitied. With Jew and Gentile alike, evil and not good, the curse and not the blessing, have been connected with the cross. In men's thought and symbols it has been treated as synonymous with ignominy and weakness and crime. God had allowed this idea to root itself universally, in order that there might be provided a place of shame, lower than all others, for the great Substitute who in the fulness of time was to take the sinner's place, and be himself the great outcast from man and God, despised and rejected, deemed unworthy even *to die* within the gates of the holy city.

Not till four thousand years had gone by did it begin to be rumored that the cross was not what men thought it, the place of the curse and shame, but of strength and honor and life and blessing. Then it was that there burst upon the astonished world the bold announcement, "God forbid that I should glory, save in the Cross of

our Lord Jesus Christ.'' Greek and Roman, Jew and
Gentile, prince, priest, philosopher, rabbi, Stoic, Epi-
curean, Pharisee, barbarian, Scythian, bond and free,
North, South, East and West, looked to one another with
contemptuous impatience, indignant at the audacity of
a few Jews thus affronting and defying the ''public
opinion'' of nations and ages; assailing the faiths and
unbeliefs of earth with this as their only sword; striking
down the idols with this as their only hammer; and with
this, as their one lever, proposing to turn the world
upside down.

From that day the Cross became a power in the earth;
a power which went forth, like the light, noiselessly yet
irresistibly; smiting down all religions alike, all shrines
alike, all altars alike; sparing no superstition or philosophy; neither flattering priesthood, nor succumbing to
statesmanship; tolerating no error, yet refusing to draw
the sword for truth; a power superhuman, yet wielded
by human, not angelic hands; ''the power of God unto
salvation.''

This power remains; in its mystery, its silence, its in-
fluence it remains. The Cross has not become obsolete;
the preaching of the Cross has not ceased to be effectual.
There are men among us who would persuade us that in
this late age the Cross is out of date and out of fashion,
time-worn, not time-honored; that Golgotha witnessed
only a common martyr scene; that the great sepulchre
is but a Hebrew tomb; that the Christ of the future and
the Christ of the past are widely different. But this
shakes us not. It only leads us to clasp the Cross more
fervently, and to study it more profoundly, as embody-
ing in itself that Gospel which is at once the wisdom
and the power of God.

Yet is the Cross not without its mysteries, or, as men would say, its puzzles, its contradictions. It illuminates, yet it darkens; it interprets, yet it confounds. It raises questions, but refuses to answer all that is raised. It solves difficulties, but it creates them too. It locks as well as unlocks. It openeth, and no man shutteth; it shutteth, and no man openeth. It is life, and yet it is death. It is honor, yet it is shame. It is wisdom, but also foolishness. It is both gain and loss; both pardon and condemnation; both strength and weakness; both joy and sorrow; both love and hatred; both medicine and poison; both hope and despair. It is grace, and yet it is righteousness. It is law, yet it is deliverance from law. It is Christ's humiliation, yet it is Christ's exaltation. It is Satan's victory, yet it is Satan's defeat. It is the gate of heaven, and the gate of hell.

Let us look at the Cross as the divine proclamation and interpretation of the things of God; the key to His character, His word, His ways, His purposes; the clue to the intricacies of the world's and the church's history.

IT IS THE INTERPRETER OF MAN

By means of it God has brought out to view what is in man. In the Cross man has spoken out. He has exhibited himself, and made unconscious confession of his feelings, especially in reference to God—to His being, His authority, His character, His law, His love.

Though "the determinate counsel and foreknowledge of God" (Acts ii. 23) were at work in the awful transaction, yet it was man who erected the cross, and nailed the Son of God to it. Permitted by God to give vent to the feelings of his heart, and placed in circumstances the least likely to call forth anything but love, he thus

expresses them in hatred of God and of His incarnate
Son. Reckoning the death of the cross the worst of all,
he deems it the fittest for the Son of the Blessed. Thus
the enmity of the natural heart speaks out, and man
not only confesses publicly that he is a hater of God,
but he takes pains to show the intensity of his hatred.
Nay, he glories in his shame, crying aloud, "Crucify
Him, Crucify Him! This is the heir; come, let us kill
Him! Not this man, but Barabbas!"

The Cross thus interpreted man, drew the mask of
pretended religion from his face, and exhibited a soul
overflowing with the malignity of hell.

You say, "I don't hate God; I may be indifferent to
Him; He may not be in all my thoughts; but I don't
hate Him."

Then what does that Cross mean? Love, hatred, indifference—which? Does love demand the death of the
loved one? Does indifference crucify its object? Look
at your hands! Are they not red with blood? Whose
blood is that? The blood of God's own Son! No:
neither love nor indifference shed that blood. It was
hatred that did it; enmity; the enmity of the carnal
mind.

You say that I have no right to judge you.

I am not judging you. It is yon Cross that judges
you, and I am asking you to judge yourself by it. It is
yon Cross that interprets your purposes, and reveals the
thoughts and intents of your heart.

Oh, what a revelation! Man hating God, and hating
most when God is loving most! Man acting as a devil,
and taking the devil's side against God!

You say, "What have I to do with that cross, and
what right have you to identify me with the crucifiers?

Pilate did it, Caiaphas did it, the Jew did it, the Roman did it; I did it not." Nay, but you did, you did. You did it in your representatives—the civilized Roman and the religious Jew; and until you come out from the crucifying crowd, disown your representatives, and protest against the deed, you are verily guilty of that blood.

"But how am I to sever myself from these crucifiers, and protest against their crime?"

By believing in the name of the Crucified One! For all unbelief is approval of the deed and identification with the murderers. Faith is man's protest against the deed, and the identification of himself, not only with the friends and disciples of the Crucified One, but with the Crucified One Himself.

The Cross, then, was the public declaration of man's hatred of God, man's rejection of His Son, and man's avowal of his belief that he needs no Savior. If anyone denies the ungodliness of humanity and pleads for the native goodness of the race, I ask, What means yon Cross? Of what is it the revealer and interpreter? Of hatred or of love? Of good or of evil?

Besides, in this *rejection* of the Son of God, we have also man's *estimate* of Him. He had been for thirty years despised and rejected, He had been valued and sold for thirty pieces of silver, a robber had been preferred to Him; but at the cross, this estimate comes out more awfully, and there we see how man undervalued His person, His life, His blood, His word. His whole errand from the Father.

"What think ye of Christ?" was God's question. Man's answer was—"THE CROSS!" Was not that as explicit as it was appalling?

As the Cross reveals man's depravity, so does it exhibit his foolishness. His condemnation of Him, in whom God delighted, shows this. His erection of the Cross shows it still more. As if he could set at naught Jehovah, and clear the earth of Him who had come down as the doer of His will! Man's attempt to cast shame on the Lord of Glory is like a child's effort to blot out or discolor the sun. And as the erection of the Cross was the revelation of his folly, so has been his subsequent estimate of it, and of the Gospel which has issued from it. He sees in it no wisdom, but only foolishness, and this ascription of foolishness to the Cross is but the more decided proof of his own foolishness. He stumbles at this stumbling-stone. The Cross is an offence to him, and the preaching of it folly.

My friend, what is that Cross to *you?* Is it folly or wisdom? Do you see, in the way of salvation which it reveals, the excellency of wisdom, as well as the excellency of power and love? Has the Cross, interpreted to you by the Holy Ghost, revealed your own heart as a hell of darkness and evil? Have you accepted its exposition of your character, and welcomed it also as salvation for the lost—reconciliation between you and God?

IT IS THE INTERPRETER OF GOD

That "the Word was made flesh" is a blessed fact, fraught with grace to us. But incarnation is not the whole of the Bible; no, not half of it. It is not at Bethlehem, but at Golgotha, that we get the full interpretation of God's character. "Unto us a child is born" is the dawn; "It is finished" is the noon. The Cross carries out and completes what the cradle began.

It is the God of grace that the Cross reveals Him.

It is love, free love, that shines out in its fulness there. "Hereby perceive we the love of God, because He laid down His life for us" (1 John iii:16). It is as "the Lord, the Lord God, merciful and gracious," that He shows Himself. Nor could any demonstration of the *sincerity* of the divine love equal this. It is love stronger than shame, and suffering, and death; love immeasurable; love unquenchable. Truly "God is love." In his treatment of the Son of God, man was putting that love to the test. In the Cross he was putting it to the extremest test to which love could be put. But it stands them all. Man's most terrible tests but draw it forth the more copiously, and give it new opportunities of displaying its riches. What more extreme test can man ask, or God give, than this?

But *righteousness* as well as grace is here. The God who spared not His own Son is "the righteous Lord who loveth righteousness," and who "will by no means clear the guilty."

We learn God's righteous character in many ways. We learn it from its dealings with righteousness, as in the case of all unfallen ones; we learn it still more fully from its dealings with sin, as in our fallen word; but we learn it most of all, from its dealings with both of these at once, and in the same person, on the cross of Christ. For here is the righteous Son of God bearing the unrighteousness of men.

How shall God both reward and punish at once; reward the righteous One, yet punish the Substitute of the unrighteous? Surely righteousness will deal mildly with sin, when found laid on One so righteous, and so beloved for His righteousness. It will mitigate the penalty, and spare the beloved One.

No, it does not! It will not admit of the principle that sin is less sin or less punishable in such circumstances. Even when found lying on the most righteous and the most beloved of all, upon the very highest Person in the universe, it must be dealt with as sin, and punished as truly as when found upon the common sinner. There must be no exemption and no mitigation.

How terrible is the righteousness of God, as interpreted by the Cross of Christ! How infinitely holy, how gloriously perfect, how inexorably just, is the God who gave His Son! His love is no weakness, no good nature, no easy indifference to wrong and right. It is righteous love; and as such the Cross proclaims it with loud and most unambiguous utterance. All the divine perfections are seen here in harmonious glory; mercy and truth; grace and justice; the perfection of holiness combined with the perfection of love. A righteous Judge and a righteous pardon! Righteousness forgiving, saving, justifying, glorifying; taking the side of law in condemning sin, yet taking the side of love in delivering the sinner himself.

O Cross of Christ, tell us more and more of this grace of God! Preach reconciliation to the alien, pardon to the guilty, assurance of God's free yet holy love to the dark and suspicious soul! Speak to our hearts, speak to our consciences, pour in light, break our bonds, heal our wounds; all by means of thy interpretation of the divine character, thy revelation of the righteous love of God!

IT IS THE INTERPRETER OF LAW

The Cross tells us that the law is holy, and just, and good; that not one jot or tittle of it can pass away. The *perfection* of the law is the message from Calvary, even more awfully than from Sinai. The *power* of law, the *vengeance* of law, the *inexorable tenacity* of law, the *grandeur* of law, the unchangeable and infrangible *sternness* of law—these are the announcements of the Cross.

Never was there so terrible a proclamation of law, and so vivid a commentary upon it, as from the Cross of Christ. In the crosses of the two thieves there was the declaration of law, but not half so explicit as in the Cross of the righteous Son of God. He who has most honored the law is the one whom the law refuses to let go; nay, whom it compels to suffer most. All His lifetime's honor of the law seems to go for nothing. It stands Him in no stead, now that He has undertaken to answer for the sinner. There is no relaxation of law in His behalf. Law—unpitying, relentless, remorseless law—demands from Him the double debt; first, the fulfilment of all its precepts, and then the endurance of its penalties as if He had fulfilled not one of its statutes, but had broken them all.

Thus by the Cross does God interpret the law to us; showing us, with divine expressiveness, what it is, and what it can do. It was law that condemned the Son of God. It was law that erected the cross, and nailed the Sin-bearer to it. It was law that afflicted Him and put Him to grief. It was law that shed His innocent blood. Surely, of all the many illustrations and interpretations which law has received in the world's history, there is none like this.

By the Cross does God protect against all attempts to destroy or dilute, to mutilate or modify the law. Man thinks it too strict, too broad; nay, affirms that Christ came to mitigate it, and to give us a salvation founded on a modified law, and obtained by our obedience to such a law. God, in the Cross of Christ, says, "I do not think so. See yon cross, and My Son upon it, bearing the law's penalty. Would I have made Him do this had it been too strict? Did He obey too much? Did He suffer too heavily?" Thus in the Cross God upholds the law as well as expounds it; protesting against the idea that the Gospel is just the law lowered and relaxed so as to suit our fallen state of being; and proclaiming to us a Gospel founded upon a fulfilled, an unmodified, an unchangeable law.

O man, read the divine comment on the law as given on the cross, and learn what sin is, and what righteousness is! Man, in erecting that cross, was no doubt making a mock both at law and at sin. He was refusing the love of God as well as the law of God. He was, like Cain, rejecting the sin offering, and saying, "I need it not." But God was exhibiting to us the reality and the darkness of sin. In the Cross, God was condemning sin, and showing how different His estimate of it was from that of man. And there is nothing so fitted to convince, to overawe, to overwhelm the sinner as the sight of that Cross. "They shall look on Me whom they have pierced, and mourn." It is the sight of the *Cross* that brings a man down to the dust, that produces genuine repentance—godly sorrow, such as law alone could not accomplish. Look, then, and be smitten to the heart by the spectacle of the Lamb of God on the tree, wounded for our transgressions, bruised for our iniquities, "made under the law," enduring the curse of the law, that from that curse we might be redeemed.

IT INTERPRETS SIN

As the interpreter of law, it is necessarily the interpreter of sin; for as "by the law is the knowledge of sin," so that which expounds the law must also discover sin. The Cross took up the ten commandments, and on each of their "Thou shalts" and "Thou shalt nots" flung such a new and divine light that sin in all its hideousness of nature and minuteness of detail stood out to view, as it never did before. "the abominable thing" which Jehovah hates.

Sin was on the earth before Sinai's thunder awoke the desert and shook the camp of Israel; but it was hidden, or but dimly seen. As the war-rocket sent at midnight shows the whole ground and camp, so did the blaze of Sinai light up the law and discover sin.

There was sin upon the earth before the Christ of God died; but it was, with all the illumination of Sinai, but imperfectly known. As the lightning of heaven, more potent and penetrating than the most brilliant war-rocket, bursting down at midnight on some plain or valley, lights up the landscape far and near, so did the heavenly glory of the Cross unfold in awful vividness and infinite detail "the exceeding sinfulness of sin."

It showed that sin was no trifle which God would overlook; that the curse was no mere threat which God could depart from when it suited Him. It showed that the standard of sin was no sliding scale, to be raised or lowered at pleasure, that the punishment of sin was no arbitrary infliction, and that its pardon was not the expression of divine indifference to its evil. It showed that sin was no variable or uncertain thing, but fixed and precise; a thing to which God was pointing His

finger and saying, "I hate *that,* and *that,* and *that.*"
It showed that the wages of sin is death, that the soul
that sinneth must die; that sin and its fruits and penalties are *certainties,* absolute certainties, before which
heaven and earth must pass away. It showed that sin
is no mere misfortune or disease, but *guilt,* which must
go before the Judge, and receive judicial doom at His
hand. It showed all these when it showed us our divine
Substitute, dying the Just for the unjust; God lowering
none of His demands, nor abating aught of His wrath,
even in the case of His belovéd Son.

The Cross showed us, moreover, that the essence of sin
is hatred of God; and that man is, by nature, just what
the apostle calls him, a "hater of God" (Rom. i. 30).

The law had told us but the one half of this. In saying, "Thou shalt love the Lord thy God," it pointed to
sin as the want of love, but that was all. The Cross
goes farther than this, and shows us sin as enmity to
God, and man as a murderer of the Lord of Glory.

Is not this a discovery of the malignity of sin such as
had never been imagined before? O what must man be
when he can hate, condemn, mock, scourge, spit upon,
crucify the Christ of God, when coming to him clothed
in love, and with the garments of salvation? And what
must *sin* be, when, in order to expiate it, the Lord of
Glory must die upon the tree, an outcast, a criminal, a
curse before God and man, before earth and heaven!

IT INTERPRETS THE GOSPEL

That good news were on the way to us was evident
from the moment that Mary brought forth her first-born
and by divine premonition called His name "JESUS."
Good will to men was then proclaimed. But the Substi-

tute had then only *commenced* His mission of grace.
Step by step the good news unfolded themselves, as He
passed over our earth, doing the deeds and speaking the
words of love. But not till the cross is erected, and the
blood is shed, and the life is taken, do we fully learn
how it is that His work is so precious, and that the
tidings concerning it furnish so glorious a Gospel.

The Gospel is good news concerning a divine Sin-
bearer; concerning that death which is everlasting life
to us; concerning that blood which purges the conscience
from dead works, cleansing from sin, and reconciling us
to God. The Cross is the bruising of the heel of the
woman's seed, and the bruising of the serpent's head;
and that is good news. The Cross is the adjustment of
every question raised by law and righteousness, by God
or by conscience; the righteous and honorable set-
tlement of every claim that can be made against the sinner; and that is good news. The Cross is the appointed
meeting-place between the sinner and God, where the
ambassadors of peace take their stand, beseeching the
wanderer to turn and live, the rebel to be reconciled to
God. There the covenant of reconciliation was sealed,
peace made, the debt paid, the ransom given. And are
not these glad tidings of great joy?

IT INTERPRETS SERVICE

We are redeemed that we may *obey*. We are set free
that we may *serve*, even as God spoke to Pharaoh, "Let
My people go, that they may serve Me." But the Cross
defined the service, and showed us its nature. It is the
service of love and liberty; yet it is also the service of
reproach, and shame, and tribulation.

We are crucified with Christ!

This brings out our position as saints. We are crucified followers of a crucified Lord. We are crucified to
the world, and the world to us, by the Cross of Christ.
But besides this, we have to take up our cross and bear
it. It is not *His* cross we bear. None but He could
bear that. It is a cross of our own, calling us to self-
denial, flesh-denial, and world-denial; pointing out to us
a path of humiliation, trial, toil, weakness, reproach,
such as our Master trod. Yes, it is a cross *of our own*
that we are to bear; not, indeed, of our own making or
seeking—for self-made, self-sought crosses are evil, not
good—but still a cross of our own. There is a personal
cross for each, which we are to take up and bear, a cross
which is the true badge of discipleship, the genuine
mark of authentic service. What He bore for us is
done; it cannot be borne over again; it is not for any
but Himself to carry. But as He had a cross to bear
for us, so have we a cross to bear for Him; and "for His
body's sake, which is the church."

In entering Christ's service, let us, then, count the
cost. In following Him, let us not shrink from the
Cross. It was His badge of service for us; let us accept
it as ours for Him.

To the world the Cross is an offense and a stumbling-
block in two ways: it makes those who have taken it up
objects of dislike to others, and it is itself an object of
dislike to these others. Thus, while it unites the saints,
it divides them from the world. It is the banner round
which the former rally and gather; it is the mark
against which the arrows of the latter are turned.

For there are "enemies of the Cross of Christ," and
enemies of Christ Himself. Of them the apostle says,
"their end is destruction." Thus the Cross is both life

and death, salvation and destruction. It is the golden
sceptre; it is the iron rod. It is the Shepherd's staff
of love; it is the Avenger's sword of fire. It is the tree
of life and cup of blessing; it is the cup of the wine of
the wrath of God.

O enemy of the Cross of Christ, know your awful
doom! Do not take refuge in fancied neutrality, rea-
soning with yourself that because you are not a scoffer or
a profligate, you are not an enemy. Remember that it
is written, "He that is not for Me is against Me," and
"The friendship of the world is enmity with God."
That cross shall be a witness against you in the day
when the Crucified One returns as Judge and King.
The early Christians had a tradition among themselves
that the cross was to be a sign of His coming, appearing
in the heavens as the herald of His advent. Whether
this is to be the case or not, the Cross in that day will
be the object of terror to its enemies. They would not
be saved by it; they shall perish by it. They would
not take its pardon; they must bear its condemnation.
The love which it so long proclaimed shall be turned
into wrath. The glorious light beaming forth from it to
light them to the kingdom of light shall then become
darkness. Their sun shall set, no more to rise. Their
night shall begin—the long eternal night that has no
dawn in prospect, and no star to break its gloom.

THE GREAT HERESY

By DAVID J. BURRELL, D. D.

In one of the boldest and most picturesque portions of Scripture we are introduced into the councils of the ineffable Trinity. The three Persons are represented as in solemn conference respecting the deliverance of our sin-stricken race. The cry of the erring and perishing has come up into their ears. The inquiry is heard:

"Whom shall we send, and who will go for us?"

Then the only begotten Son offers Himself: "Here am I; send me!"

He girds Himself with omnipotence, binds upon His feet the sandals of salvation, and goes forth as a knight-errant to vindicate and rescue the children of men.

When next we behold Him, He is a child, wrapped in swaddling-clothes and lying in a manger. The incarnation is the first chapter in His great undertaking, and a necessary part of it. As Anselm says, "He must become man in order to suffer, and He must continue to be God in order that He may suffer enough for all." In thus assuming our nature He laid aside the form of His Godhood and "the glory which He had with the Father before the world was"; but He never lost sight of His beneficent purpose. He realized constantly that He had come to redeem the world by dying for it.

In one of the earliest pictures of the nativity He is represented as lying in the manger, while just above Him, on the wall of the stable, is the shadow of a cross. So Holman Hunt paints Him in the carpenter shop. The day's work is over. The spent Toiler lifts His arms

110

in an attitude of utter weariness, and the level rays of the setting sun cast upon the wall yonder again the shadow of a cross. The suggestion is true. He was born under that shadow and lived under it. He knew that He had come to die. He knew that, inasmuch as the penalty had been passed upon the race, "The soul that sinneth, it shall die," there could be no deliverance but by death.

Out in the wilderness, after the forty days of fasting, the adversary met Jesus and presented to His weak and suffering soul the great temptation. He led Him to a high place, and with a wave of the hand, directed His thought to all the kingdoms of this world, saying:

"All these are mine. I know Thy purpose. Thou art come to win this world by dying for it. Why pay so great a price? I know Thy fear and trembling—for Thou art flesh—in view of the nails, the fever, the dreadful exposure, the long agony. *Why pay so great a price?* I am the prince of this world. One act of homage, and I will abdicate! Fall down and worship me!"

Never before or since has there been such a temptation, so specious, so alluring. But Jesus had covenanted to die for sinners. He knew there was really no other way of accomplishing salvation for them. He could not be turned aside from the work which He had volunteered to do. Therefore He put away the alluring suggestion with the word:

"Get thee behind Me, Satan! I cannot be moved. I know the necessity that is laid upon Me. I know that My way to the kingdom is only by the Cross. I am therefore resolved to suffer and die for the deliverance of men."

Let us look again. Jesus was on His last journey
to Jerusalem—that memorable journey of which it is
written, "He set His face steadfastly" toward the
Cross. He had been with His disciples now three years,
but had not been able to fully reveal His mission, because they were not strong enough to bear it. A man
with friends, yet friendless, lonely in the possession of
His great secret, He had longed to give them His full
confidence, but dared not venture. Now, as they journeyed southward through Cæsarea Philippi, He asked
them:

"Who do men say that I am?"

And they answered, "Some say John the Baptist;
some, Elias; others, Jeremias, or one of the prophets."

And He saith, "But who say ye that I am?"

Then Peter—brave, impulsive, glorious Peter—witnessed his good confession:

"Thou art the Christ, the Son of the living God."

The hour had come! His disciples were beginning
to know Him. He would give them His full confidence.
So as they journeyed toward Jerusalem He told them
all—how He had come to redeem the world by bearing
its penalty of death. "He began to show them how He
must suffer many things of the elders and chief priests
and scribes, and be killed."

At that point Peter could hold his peace no longer,
but began to rebuke Him, saying:

"Be it far from Thee, Lord! To suffer? To die?
Nay, to reign in Messianic splendor!"

And Jesus turning, said unto Peter, "Get thee behind
Me, Satan!"—the very words with which He had re-
pelled the same suggestion in the wilderness. As He
looked on His disciple He saw not Peter, but Satan—

perceived h⌐w the adversary had for the moment taken possession, as it were, of this man's brain and conscience and lips. "Get thee behind Me, Satan! I know thee; I recognize thy crafty suggestion; but I am not to be turned aside from My purpose. Get thee behind Me! Thou a⌐t an offence unto Me. Thy words are not of divine wisdom, but of human policy. Thou savorest not the things that be of God, but those that be of men!"

THE VITAL CENTER OF CHRISTIANITY

We are now ready for our proposition, which is this: *The vicarious death of Jesus is the vital center of the whole Christian system; and any word which contravenes it is in the nature of a satanic suggestion.*

There is one truth before which all other truths whatsoever dwindle into relative insignificance, to wit, that our Lord Jesus Christ was wounded for our transgressions and bruised for our iniquities, that by His stripes we might be healed. The man who apprehends this by faith, is saved.

THE GREAT HERESY

And contrariwise, any denial of this truth is mortal heresy. The first santanic suggestion made to man was a denial of the law, when the tempter said to Adam, "Thou shalt not surely die." The last satanic suggestion is a denial of grace: "It is not necessary that Christ should die for thee." The first ruined the race, and the last will destroy any man who entertains it.

The suggestion comes in various ways, as when it is said that the Gospel is not the only religion that saves: "If a man is sincere, what difference does it make? Here is a Confucianist bowing before his ancestral tablets; here is a Brahman bathing in his sacred river;

and here an African bowing before his fetish. All
these are sincere. Shall they not be saved with us?"

If so, then the death of the Lord Jesus Christ, the
only begotten Son of the Father, was an incomprehen-
sible waste of divine resource, and there is no signifi-
cance in the word that is written, "There is none other
name under heaven given among men, whereby we
must be saved."

It is said again, that we are saved by the life of the
Lord Jesus Christ as an example of holiness, leading us
on to self-culture and character-building; and His death
has practically nothing to do with our entrance into life.

If that is true, then Christ did but mock our infirmity
in setting up such an ideal. He did indeed come into
the world to tell us how men ought to live, what a true
man ought to be, what character means. That was in-
cidental to His great redemptive mission, leading us on
from deliverance to holiness. But if that were all, then
I say He mocked our infirmity, for there is not an
earnest man who does not kneel down beside his bed at
night, after his most strenuous effort to imitate Christ,
and say, "Have mercy upon me, O Lord, for I have
sinned." We have all sinned and come short of the
glory of God.

Again, it is said that Christ did not die vicariously,
under the burden of sin, taking our place before the
offended law, but died as all martyrs die. "He came
into the world as a reformer, to overthrow the evil conditions of things, and suffered the fate of all earnest
souls. He gathered into His devoted heart the shafts
of the adversary, and fell."

If that be so, what is the meaning of the constant statement that the death of Jesus Christ was a voluntary

death? The Father gave Him, He gave Himself, an offering for sin. "I have power to lay down My life, and I have power to take it again; no man taketh My life from Me." Life was His, He made it, He played with it as little children play with their toys.

1. *To deny this doctrine of the vicarious atonement, in any of these ways or otherwise, is to set one's self athwart the whole trend of Scripture.*

From Genesis to Revelation there is a thoroughfare stained with the blood that cleanseth from sin. No sooner had man sinned than the protevangel spoke of the "seed of the woman" suffering for sin. The first altar, reared by the closed gate of paradise, prophesied of the slain Lamb of God. As the years passed, the prophets declared, with ever increasing clearness and particularity, the coming sacrifice. David sang of it in his Messianic psalms. Isaiah drew the portrait of the agonizing Christ as if He had gazed on the cross: "He is . . . a Man of sorrows, and acquainted with grief . . . Surely He hath borne our griefs, and carried our sorrows. . . . And the Lord hath laid on Him the iniquity of us all." The same truth was emphasized by Moses, Daniel, Zechariah, all the prophets down to Malachi, who, waving his torch in the twilight of the long darkness which closed the old economy, said, "The Sun of righteousness shall arise with healing in His wings." Open the Book where you will, the face of Jesus, "so marred more than any man's," yet divinely beautiful, looks out upon you.

The rites and symbols of the Old Testament all find their fulfilment in Christ crucified. Their centre was the tabernacle. Enter it and observe how it is everywhere sprinkled with blood. Here is blood flowing down the brazen altar, blood on the ewer, the golden candlestick, the table of shewbread, the altar of incense; blood on the floor, the ceiling; on posts and pillars, on knops and blossoms, everywhere. Lift the curtain and pass into the holiest of all—but not without blood on your palms. Here is blood on the ark of the covenant, blood on the mercy-seat—blood, blood everywhere. What does it mean? Nothing, absolutely nothing, unless it declares the necessity of the Cross. It is an empty dumb show, except as it points the worshiper to Him whose vicarious death is the only means of our salvation.

Wherefore, I say, the man who denies this truth must set himself against the sum and substance of the Scriptures. For if the atoning death of Christ be taken out of that blessed Book, it is, as a solution of the great problem of life, of no more value than a last year's almanac.

THE TESTIMONY OF HISTORY

2. Again, *a denial of this doctrine involves a downright rejection of the philosophy of history.*

The world has been growing better ever since the cross first cast its luminous shadow over it. Progress is a fact—a fact that must be accounted for. Hume undertook to write history without Christ, and found it a labyrinth without a clue. So did Gibbon. They saw civilization advancing through the centuries; but, rejecting Christ, they could perceive no reason for it. The "logic of events" was nothing to them. There can, indeed, be no "philosophy of history" for a man who refuses to see Constantine's cross in the heavens, with its great prophecy, "In this sign thou shalt conquer." It is a miraculous coincidence that the limits of civilization on earth to-day are coextensive with the charmed circle known as *Christendom*. "The world before Christ," says Luthardt, "was a world without love." The church with the proclamation of Chrisit, and Him crucified, has come down through the centuries like Milton's angel with the torch; and all along the way have sprung up institutions of learning and charity and righteousness. The Cross is the vital power of civilization. "All the light of sacred story," and of secular story as well, "gathers round its head sublime." If the world grows better, it is because Christ died for it.

THE UNIVERSAL INSTINCT OF MANKIND

3. Still further, *to deny the vital importance of the vicarious death of Jesus is to contradict the universal instinct of mankind.*

The doctrine of the redemptive power of substitutionary pain is not our exclusive property. It has a place in all, or nearly all, the false religions. It may be dimly seen in the hammer of Thor; in the wounded foot of Brahma treading on the serpent; in the fable of Prometheus, bound to the Caucasus with a vulture at his vitals, and lamenting, "I must endure this until one of the gods shall bear it for me." It is still more evident in the institution of the sacrifice. Wherever a living thing is slain upon the altar, it means vicarious expiation, or else it means nothing at all.

And why should it be thought strange that God should send His only begotten Son to suffer in our stead? Is not *sympathy* the noblest as well as the com-

monest thing in human experience? Men are suffering everywhere and always for other men. Parents are
suffering for their children. The pains which we all
endure are, for the most part, not the consequence of
our own acts. At this point of sympathy our nature
reaches its noblest and best. We esteem, above all, the
unselfish man who voluntarily bears the burdens of
others. Should we not, then, expect something of the
same sort in our Father? He made us in His likeness.
It would be monstrous if God did not sympathize with
His children who have fallen into trouble. The Cross
is the very highest expression of sympathy in the universe. The atonement is what we should expect. It
is just like God.

And it is God's exact response to the universal need.
It fits our circumstances. As Coleridge said, "The
Gospel finds me." It answers the deepest longing of
earnest souls. Dr. Chamberlain relates that among those
converted by his preaching at the sacred city of Benares
was a devotee who had dragged himself many miles
upon his knees and elbows to bathe in the Ganges. He
had at the bottom of his heart the common conviction
of sin and desire of cleansing.

"If I can but reach the Ganges," he thought, "this
shame and bondage and fear will be taken away."

Weak and emaciated from his long pilgrimage, he
dragged himself down to the river's edge, and, praying
to Gunga, crept into it; then, withdrawing, he lay upon
the river's bank and moaned:

"The pain is still here!"

At that moment he heard a voice from the shadow of
a banyan tree near by. It was the missionary telling
the story of the Cross. The devotee listened, drank it

in, rose to his knees, then to his feet; then, unable to restrain himself, he clapped his hands and cried:

"That's what I want! That's what I want!"

It is what we all want. The whole creation has from time immemorial groaned and travailed for it.

And it is our only hope. There are other religions and other philosophies, but none that suggests a rational plan of pardon for sin. I remember an old crucifix, in the public square of a Brittany village, which no one passed without bending the knee. Workmen on their way to the fields, little children goin to school, all bowed before that stone figure of the Christ, which the storms of centuries had worn almost out of human semblance. The last night, as I was leaving the village in the twilight, I saw an old woman bent almost prostrate before it. Her hands were clasped; her uplifted face bore the marks of suffering. I could not know the bitterness of that poor heart, but her eyes were turned toward the infinite Source of help and consolation. The dear hand upon the cross lifts every burden, heals every wound, and saves us from the penalty, the shame, and the bondage of sin.

And this is why we preach Christ, and Him crucified. "There is none other name under heaven given among men, whereby we must be saved." "He was wounded for our transgressions, He was bruised for our iniquities; . . . and with His stripes we are healed." He is thus made unto us wisdom and righteousness and sanctification and redemption. He is first, last, midst, and all in all.

WILLIE LEAR, THE SUBSTITUTE

By D. W. WHITTLE

Willie Lear lived near Palmyra, Missouri. In 1862 he was a young man of about 18 years of age. Like most of those who lived in his neighborhood, he sympathized with the South in the civil war which was at that time in progress. The Union forces occupied Palmyra, and had control of the district. Outrages were committed on both sides, and many indefensible deeds are recorded in the local histories of those sad times. Union soldiers were shot down from behind hedges, and Union men were driven away from their homes, and sometimes foully treated. To avenge these things, and to check them, the Federal commander arrested and imprisoned a large number of the citizens. They were all charged with being "guerillas," and, after trial by court-martial, were all sentenced to be shot. Willie Lear was among the number.

After this condemnation, the general decided to select ten of the number of those condemned for immediate execution, and reserve the remainder under hope of pardon if outrages in the neighborhood ceased, or for future punishment if not. These ten were drawn by lot. Willie Lear was not of this number.

A neighbor of Lear's, who was among the number to be shot, was terribly distressed at the thought of his situation. He was the father of a large family, a poor man, and the thought of the helpless condition in which he would leave his loved ones was very distressing to him.

Lear saw all this, and it deeply moved him. He stepped forward to the commanding officer and offered *to take his neighbor's place*. The officer had no objection. The order had been issued that ten men of the number should be shot, and if that number was made up, the law would be satisfied. The neighbor with the deepest gratitude accepted Lear as his substitute; and so, by the acquiescence of the three parties concerned, the representative of the law, the condemned by the law, and the satisfier of the law by substitution, the matter was settled.

Willie Lear took the place of his friend in line with the nine men drawn up before a detachment prepared with loaded rifles, and at the command, "Fire!" he, with the others, fell, riddled with bullets, his blood soaking the earth.

As the man for whom he died looked upon that blood, and beheld that mangled body what would be his thought? Would he not say, with streaming eyes:

"He died for me. I owe my life to him. O that I could do anything to show my gratitude to one who has done so much for me!"

If he were asked, "How is it that you are delivered from the sentence that was hanging over you?" would he be apt to ignore the work of his substitute by magnifying the importance of some fancied work of his own in the acceptance of the substitute? Would he say, "Oh, I was saved by my faith, and by my determination to live a better life? It is all by faith and the development of character." Would he have been so ungrateful as to leave out all mention of the death of that noble young man in his stead as the alone cause of his escape? If he would, he was not worth dying for, and it was a curse to his family and the community that he was spared. But no. He never returned such answers. He could not treat the act of his friend with such indifference.

Men for whom Christ died on the cross talk that way; but this man never did. He never tired of telling of how Willie Lear had saved him, and gladly acknowledged his obligation to him.

Reader, do you believe that Jesus Christ died for your sins? Do you believe that because He died for your sins, and you have accepted Him, your sins are forgiven? Believing in Him, are you confessing Him, and striving to show your gratitude by a life consecrated to His service? Oh! let us us who are Christ's never tire of telling the story of the redemption by His blood; let us never rob Him of His glory as our alone Savior and Redeemer by attributing our salvation from sin and our hope of eternal life to anything else than His death upon the cross for our sins.

We greatly err when we think that any other Gospel, or any other form of the Gospel, will be more successful in reaching men, no matter what they are or who they are. No man can be saved without the power of God being put forth to save him; and as God has decreed that "the preaching of the Cross is the power of God," we must, if we would see men saved, preach the Cross. And the meaning of that is, "This is My blood, which is shed for many for the remission of sins." Christ is the sinner's Substitute.